The Creativity Myth

A New Systems Design Paradigm for the 21st Century and Beyond

By

Dr. Raymond Leslie Newkirk

The best Creativity Myth that I have ever heard is that Human Beings are creative. This is because Humanity can engage in many arguments for no good reason. This demands great Creativity. Especially if they they win their arguments.

About the Author

Dr. Raymond Leslie Newkirk, Psy.D., Ph.D., Ph.D., Th. C., F.B.I.M., C.Q.A

Founder, Entrepreneur, Product Architect, Inventive Problem Solver, Virtual-Learning Pioneer, Deep Technology Scientist, Thought Leader, Consultant, Mentor, Publisher Author, Speaker, Internationally Ranked Athlete and Record Holder.

Dr. Raymond Leslie Newkirk is an internationally respected consulting specialist having earned advanced degrees and certifications in several disciplines including Ph.Ds. in the Philosophy of Science and Behavioral Science, Psy.D. in Clinical Psychology, Th.C., in Theology and the Ph.D. with Distinction in Human Science. Dr. Newkirk originated the Ulthule™ approach to human performance and the Applied Intuitive Solutions Inventive Problem-Solving Knowledge Base System. His professional background includes a distinguished career in multicultural research, human system design, and executive development. He has presented the Keynote Address to global audiences.

He is the Founder & CEO of the Systems Management Institute, a firm that applies human systems design to the building of high-performance organizations. He was Founder and Chairman of Bay University, an innovative E-Learning Company. He has enjoyed a life-long interest in business and enterprise incubation. He founded his first company at the age of 16, a janitorial service with three employees, and has organized start-ups & joint ventures ever since.

Dr. Newkirk has served in diverse industries and executive capacities. He was a Senior Fellow of the Monterey Bay Management Group. He served as Chief Operating Officer of Mindmaker, Inc. of San Jose, California, an early A/I and neural net pioneer that won Best of Comdex two years consecutively during the dot.com revolution in Silicon Valley. He also served as President and Chief Operating Officer of P.Q. Information Group, b.v. the Netherlands, an innovative company that pioneered Business Rules processing software development, and Founder of the International Association of Information Management.

He led projects for the Minister of Defense and Aviation and the Royal Saudi Naval Forces for the Kingdom of Saudi Arabia and for the Office of the President, Republic of the Philippines. Dr. Newkirk has led industry-changing engagements for Southwest Bell, Bank of America, and Dell Computers. He was a VIP Priority Guest of the CNN World Business Development Congress. He was invited as a visiting Ambassador in Business Development and Technology Transfer to the Soviet Union and as an expert guest to development conferences in

Cairo, Egypt and Oxford, England. He conducted seminars for Technology Transfer, Rome, I.B.C. London and Amsterdam and S.I.B.C. Jeddah, Kingdom of Saudi Arabia.

Dr. Newkirk never stops writing. A prolific writer, he has published more than 1,600 articles, monographs, books, e-learning courses, blogs, and guest columns for the San Francisco Examiner. His latest book, Navigating Sociopaths at Work, will be available early in 2020. His most recent book, Leading by Design, has become a widely sought collector's book that is available through the Systems Management Institute Press. His next book series, Ray Newkirk Tackles Workplace Relationships, advances a fresh look at leadership thinking and establishes the foundation for a new science of Leadership. He has authored works in English, Italian, Russian, Arabic, and Latin.

He is the producer of the Ray Newkirk Library Series. He advocates the intellectual, physical, and spiritual development of the person. He studied philosophy as a Benedictine Monk in Italy and studied theology with the Franciscan Friars in Washington D.C.

He participated for many years with the Amateur Athletic Union (AAU) both as a competitor and supporter. Early in his athletic career, he attained international ranking in Olympic Weightlifting having won 12 championships and set 22 competitive records in the sport. He won Outstanding Weightlifter Award, Ohio State A.A.U. A few of his many records still stand today. Currently, he is in training to compete in the Masters World Championships and was the reigning Pacific Weightlifting Association Masters Champion where he is still in the business of chasing records.

As an amateur explorer, Ray went diving in the Red Sea, mountain climbing in Alaska, worked as a deck hand on Dutch freighter, sailed in the Bahamas, and enjoyed deep-sea fishing in the Caribbean, among other global adventures.

Dr. Newkirk is an innovative social thinker. He is concerned about the problems facing the elderly in this technological and fast paced age. He has conducted workshops for senior citizens & executives on health, nutrition, and stress management. He established a health clinic and medical network for the elderly. He also contributed to the establishment of an orphanage in the Third World, funded fellowships for students in Eastern Europe to travel abroad and participate in seminars and professional training, and established a Southeast Asian International Fellowship.

Dr. Newkirk's Guiding Perspective is:

Life, Love, Leadership, Growth, & Honor

"Live life fully. Love deeply with wisdom.

Lead others to great achievement.

Grow spiritually and intellectually.

Honor God in all I do."

Other Books by Dr. Raymond Leslie Newkirk

Additional Titles by Author

*Adventures in Paleo-Leadership

*Leading by Design

Enjoy Your Relationships

Understanding Psychotherapy

*Insider Threat Prevention

The Psychology of Insider Threat Prevention

Serious Spirituality

Adventures in Living a God Inspired Life

A God Inspired Life

Dr. Raymond Leslie Newkirk on Who We Are

From Confusion to Clarity

Cosmic Truth God, Us, and Them

*Forever Forward Becoming a Type 1 Civilization

A Person Passing By

Love All Around

Coaching Insights of Dr. Ray

Mastering the Psychology of ATICS Project Analysis

21St Century Executive Life

* Refers to a Series

Dedication

Dedicated To a Person Very Special,

To Someone Very Cheerful,

Graced With an Endearing Smile,

Divinely Supportive, and Wonderfully Patient.

With All My Love

Dedicated to My Wife - Felicisima Calma-Newkirk

The Best Friend and Wife Any Man Could Ever Have.

To Fall in Love with God

Is The Greatest of All Romances

To Seek Him

Is The Greatest of All Adventures!

To Find Him

Is The Greatest Human Achievement!

Fr. M. Raphael Simon, O.C.S.O., M.D.

(Trappist Monk)

Table of Contents

The Pursuit, Knowledge And

Belief In Truth

Is The Sovereign Good

Of The Human Race

In The Great Room of The United States
Library of Congress

Design

Preface

"The Creativity Myth" is an interesting title because many people throughout Human History appear to be very CREATIVE. How could Human Creativity ever be seen as a Myth? This is certainly a bold statement and even a bolder title for a book. Don't you think? Let us pause for a moment and take a look. So, what have we been told about creativity?

We are told that Creativity is a global human capacity for originality and newness. Out with the old and in with the new in many different ways and in many different areas of interest from Science to the Arts. Creativity is about doing something better; but is can also end up meaning doing something worse. After all, worse is creative and can also be new, but not better. Historically, some creative ideas have been terrible for Humanity. Think Nuclear Weapons. These weapons were certainly unique and also useful for their intended purpose. They solved World War II.

Now, of course, we have the Internet and it has assisted many people with initiating their new enterprises that solved many kinds of different problems, and also initiated many more new problems. Life is like this – out with the old problems and in with the new problems. How creative. Simply wonderous. Human Imagination often works in overtime and in overdrive. Imagine that. Although it is often unfortunate for doing so, Humanity is very good at using its mind to picture things that it cannot see.

I have worked with many problem-solvers in organizations who were indeed very, very good at solving the wrong problems with in-depth novelty. These people presented new solutions to old problems so they could contract on finding solutions to the new problems they created by solving the old problems that were less costly than the new problems created to solve the old problems. We are told that Creativity is omnipresent in human endeavors because creativity is a natural human power, a common behavior so to speak. Ouch and ouch again. Can this possibly be true? Is this the Case for Creativity? If so, let me ask: Where Did Creativity begin? More to the point, where did Human Creativity begin? When did Humanity become creative? How did Humanity become Creative?

Did Creativity exist before Humanity or did Humanity create Creativity? When we go by to the Beginning, we begin to understand that Creativity is actually a Theological Word. Afte all, we became "Creatures" on earth through no act of our own. Right? Speaking Mystically, and Theologically, to Create means to "make from no-thing". Obviously, this is the Province of Divinity where to create means to make from no-thing, meaning nothing. Creativity did not begin with Humanity. We the people began our work on Mother earth with something.

Our creation began before we appeared. We began from nothing that is earthly. In its raw meaning, its unadulterated nothing, to create mean to make from nothing. We human being who populate Mother Earth do not make anything from nothing. We are designers. We are arrangers. We are mixers. We are weighers. We are listeners. We are people who remember. We are innovators. We are weighers. We are sensers. We are tasters. We are commentators. We are investigators. We are painters. We are arrangers. We are lifters and movers. We re all of these things, and even more than this. Nevertheless, we are all of these things with something that preceded us. We do not make from nothing. We do not create. We arrange and we differentiate. We complete what others have initiated. We extend the existing. We nearly perfect the imperfect. We multiply. We subtract. We di so much. But, nevertheless, we do not make from nothing. Our ideas alone are Never Enough!

Introduction: Some Definitions and Descriptions

In earlier works, I suggested that Creativity in any real sense as the term implies, is a myth. I reasoned that when the authorities today speak or write about creativity, they really mean design. Doubtlessly, human beings do participate in creative-like activity, and this activity does indeed produce something new. But participating in the production of something new does not in itself provide prima facie evidence that the new product indeed results from creativity. On closer examination, it becomes obvious that in our everyday earthly experience "creators: derived new products from something else previously existing, albeit in much different form. Therefore, when many authorities speak of creativity, they mean the simple rearrangement or transformation of a previously or already existing something or other into some new emergent reality or something or other.

As has been pointed out in other papers, the transformation of something old into something new occurs more through design than authentic creativity as in a something out of nothing experience. In our earthly experience, and as far as we can determine according to human reason, Purposeful Human Activity Systems engage in design. On the other hand, and according to the workings of the human capacity for faith which forms the foundation of all human knowledge, Creativity exists as a Divine Entitative Attribute not shared in directly by homo sapiens. To understand why this must be so, and to understand at the rational level why I so strongly reason that creativity is design, we need to take a closer look at the process of design itself.

We have already seen why creativity is design examining the definition of creativity and the logical rules essential to the formulation of any definition. Now we do well to close the loop. This of course means that we need to go even deeper by examining Design itself. In this way, I can better make my case by not only discussing the aspects of creativity which make creativity design but also by looking at design itself and demonstrating that design is what the authorities really have in mind when they speak about creativity - while all the time holding out that creativity and design make strange bedfellows because creativity is a myth.

In accordance with the task now set out for us here, I will conduct the deeper examination of design by considering several of its most relevant aspects. As with creativity, this examination will also begin with a survey of design definitions. Following from this foundation, Section Two will explore other domains relevant to an understanding of design. A few such domains will include: systems of design, spaces of design, approaches to design, design models, and so forth.

However, before we can proceed with any exploration into the systems of design, we must stop and refresh our understanding of systems in general, and human activity systems in particular. Hopefully, by the time we get to the third section of this work, we will see that an adequate understanding of design must include a collective picture of design in terms of design products, design processes and design persons, i.e. designers, all as vital components of a single design system. Any attempt to understand design by exploring merely the designer, or the product, or the process separately as ends in themselves, as is often the case in creativity research, suggests a reductionistic approach inappropriate to a fuller understanding of design. And such an approach becomes a formula for failure. The author submits that an exploration into design signifies a Design Inquiry.

Therefore, as such, for the sake of effectiveness, the design exploration, our design inquiry, requires a Systems Thinking Perspective. Approaches to creativity research discussed in elsewhere are often directed and controlled by the reductionistic paradigm, as we have seen. This paradigm in itself remains forever insufficient to meet the demands of the various systems- based inquiries such as Design Inquiry, which is actually a creativity inquiry if we now understand that creativity is design. In my view, Design Inquiry springs forth from the Systems Perspective and is derived, as we shall soon discover, at least implicitly from the various definitions given for design.

Definitions of Design

Just as Guilford reported that by 1950 not much had happened in creativity research (Barron & Harrington, 1981), Gasparski further tells us that not much was done on design (1984). To demonstrate this takes only a short visit to the nearest university library, to review the catalogued entries under 'Design'. The result of such a test is remarkable: more than eight out of ten items (books, articles, etc.) are devoted to designs, i.e., they are sources of knowledge for design. And of the remainder, only a few are sources of knowledge on design Gasparski, (1984, pg. i.).

There was substantial activity about design such as the design of buildings through architectural design, but little if nothing on design itself. Also, just like creativity research, design research focuses on the design process, the designer, or the design product. Hence, just as in creativity, we are likewise showered with a great variety of design definitions. Such a multiplicity of definitions is to be expected, though, because the challenge of defining design is no less difficult a task than the one undertaken when defining creativity. Gasparski informs us when speaking of the effort to define design: "As it turns out, this is by no means a simple task, contrary to all appearances" (1984. p.

1). Gasparski goes on to suggest that a shift in paradigm (1984, p. 3) reveals the key behind the definition of design. The author previously argued for the same shift as the key to understanding creativity. Previously, in Section one, I suggested that an under- standing of the questions surrounding creativity required the adoption of the Systems Perspective, i.e., the systems paradigm. Gasparski mirrored a similar view for design when we wrote:

The overall approach to design activities characteristic of the modern concept of design, is not accidental; neither is it a rare occurrence in the modern approach to other kinds of activity. On the contrary, it is a consequence of the modern treatment of human activity. This sort of treatment has become possible owing to the dissemination of a much broader concept, called the systems approach. The generality of the approach to design is a direct manifestation of this concept: design is treated as a system, i.e. as a system including both that which is being designed, and the designing "who" or "what". Accordingly, both components of design mentioned above are defined as the Designed System and the Designing System. The design process is considered, in turn, as a manifestation of systematizing influence of the designing system on the designed systems (imposing relations):

This influence determines the designing method (methods) (Gasparski, 1984. p. 7).

Hence, the systems perspective as applied to design permits one to focus on the designer, the product and the process of design simultaneously as part of a larger system, the Suprasystem. The Reductionistic Paradigm, that used by many creativity thinkers, does just the opposite. Thus, such creativity authorities seek to define only the process, or the product, or the creative person, rather than all three together as components of a larger system.

In the previous section, the author brought out the fact that many authorities in creativity view creativity as the bringing into reality of something new. Gasparski makes a similar claim about design when he writes: "We have written above that design activity of its very essence is an informational preparation of a change of the reality" (1984, p. 7). Gasparski goes on to identify the various types of changes as either objective or subjective; intended or unintended; rational or irrational; positive utility or negative utility or non-dychotomically changes with different degrees of effectiveness; inadmissible changes; esthetically positive or negative changes, and so forth. (pp. 7-8). Hence, Gasparski presents a picture of design as an activity that seeks to change reality, consciously or unconsciously. Do not the creativity authorities suggest the same argument when they assert that creativity is as May states: "bringing something new into existence" (Davis, 1986, p. 19)?

As Gasparski would have it, we all are designers: "For, on the one hand, we are all assuredly designers: we design objects or ventures, we design processes, we design the form and we design the substance which fills this form" (1984, p. 2). The same has been argued for creativity. We are all "creative"; we "create" objects or ventures, we "create" processes, we "create" the form and we "create" the substance which fills this form. Doubtlessly, the apparently universal existence of design as a common aspect of human existence leads one to conclude with Gasparski that "there is some pandesignism" (1984, p. 2) a foot in the world. Perhaps creativity and design are indeed the same? Perhaps, we simply need a systems view to see it? After making his arguments about the need for a new paradigm, the systems paradigm, to understand the authentic essence of design, Gasparski submits the following design definition:

> Design is not an activity with just one purpose to be achieved. Design is a multi-goaled, heterotelic activity, and therefore could be analyzed as a social phenomenon, from as many points of view as possible" (Gaspasrski, 1984, p. 112).

Actually, this is a pretty good definition of design. Especially when we consider the definitions offered for creativity earlier. And in several ways, Gasparski's definition approaches a logically correct form. But what do others say about design? How do they define it? In Gasparski's case, we have a theory first and then this leads to a definition. But what about the other design authorities? Do they share Gasparski's vision?

An important point made by Gasparski, and an interesting one at that, is that the traditional view of the world naturally led to many definitions of design: "At first glance it seems that the traditional point of view leads to a great number of definitions of design, to be exact to as many as there are distinguishable designed objects" (1984, p. 3). Such was the problem with creativity. Keeping this in mind, we will now survey a few additional design definitions and see if Gasparski stands correct, that is, we will see if so many definitions exist because they evolved from "the traditional point of view". The first one is easy. Jantsch clearly addresses design as a process of human systems. Such a vision certainly does not perpetuate the traditional ideology:

> "Human systems have memories which hold not only images from the past but also images of the future which introduce the most powerful fluctuations upsetting any mechanistic stability. These images of the future play an important role in a type of autocatalytic process I shall call the human design process (Jantsch, 1975).

In a similar way, Mathur visualizes design as a conscious realization that something needs to be changed:

> The entire activity from the stage of realization of a need for change to translating the image of the future system into reality is termed design (1978).

Here Mathur hints at a method of design which includes conceptualization and modeling. Moreover, he is stating that design is concerned with the development of a future system. Unfortunately, though, in this definition, too much remains in the "fog zone", that area where ambiguity rules the day. With only this definition to go on, this author remains unsure of Mathur's basic point of view - for Mathur's definition violates the rules of definition formulation given earlier.

Other definitions fail to do any better. After thinking about them for a short time, one is forced to conclude that in many respects what is passed off as an actual definition of design, unfortunately, at its best, remains nothing more than a nominal definition. And as we have already seen, a nominal definition is really no definition at all. As an example, consider the following group of design definitions, all taken from an exploratory project with Bela Banathy, Ph.D. serving as Principal Investigator (Banathy, 1984, pp. 1-2 thru 1-4). So, what is design:

1. Conscious Design: the deliberate manipulation of the world for desired ends (Lynch, 1960).

1. Design is the conscious effort to impose meaningful order (Papanek, 1972).

1. It is the process of originating (Klir & Valach, 1967). It is all about finding the right physical components of a physical structure (Alexander, 1963).

1. Design is a goal-directed problem-solving activity (Archer, 1966).

1. Design is Decision-Making in the face of uncertainty with high penalties for error (Asimow, 1962).

1. Engineering Design is the use of scientific principles, technical information and imagination in the definition of a system to perform specific functions with maximum economy and efficiency (Eder, 1966).

1. Design is the optimum solution to their sum of the needs of a particular set of circumstance (Matchett, 1968).

1. Design is concerned with how things ought to be. The designer devises a course of action aimed at changing existing situations into preferred ones (Simon, 1969).

1. Design is the process of originating systems and predicting their fulfillment of given objectives (Sless, 1978).
    a. The purpose of systems engineering is to develop policies for management, direction, control, and regulation of activities relative to forecasting, planning, development, production, and operation of total systems to maintain overall integrity and integration as related to performance and reliability (Sage, 1977).

1. Design is a creative activity—it involves bringing into being something new and useful that has not existed previously (Reswick, 1965).

1. Design is a creative and stimulating activity, often as much akin to art and architecture as to science (Beakley & Chilton, 1974),

1. Organizational Design is the allocation of resources and people and the structuring of the organizations to carry out its objectives. The design of the organization ideally is

constructed to fit the nature of the organization' environment.

1. Organizational Learning develops the knowledge for organizational decision makers so that they can develop the organizational strategy that is responsive to the particular task environment the organization faces. Learning provides accurate information regarding appropriate design given the nature of the environment (Duncan & Weiss, 1979).

1. The designer intends to change a segment of the universe. His or her motivation is consequential action, not understanding or explanation. He or she worries about the potential effects of what he or she proposes to do. A person designs whenever he or she has a purpose in mind and devises a scheme to accomplish this purpose. The outcome of design is not the accomplishment of the purpose, but a plan for its accomplishment (Rittel, 1973).

1. Design is the technique of specifying material requirements and/or performance standards for constructing an operating part or component—specifications that are compatible with defined functions to be performed for stated parts of the system (Corrigan & Kaufman, 1966).

1. Design-as-process: Design at the scale of being does not have a goal. It's a question of living, not of planning life-not-yet-lived. Design without a product? The idea seems nonsense if applied to designing by professionals. But, seen as part of a historic shift from product thinking to process thinking, isn't it what we overlooked? Designing disappears; it becomes a way of using, an enlivening of how we live. There is no outcome.

1. Design is a question of being the architecture of process. Design is the architecture of what is happening—the architecture of being (Jones, 1970).

1. Design is the process of originating (Klir & Valach, 1967).

1. Design is concerned with making things that people want, with building up patterns which have value (Gregory, 1966).

1. Design is the imaginative jump from present facts to future possibilities (Page, 1966).

A less than cursory analysis of these definitions reveals that they focus on three principal areas, just like creativity. These are:

- Product
- Process
- Person.

Moreover, they cross the boundaries of two separate paradigms, the reductionistic, i.e., the traditional, and the systemic. To quote Banathy: "The authors represent a variety of design fields, including:

- Architecture
- Engineering
- Environmental Design
- Industrial Design
- Organizational Design
- Art
- Social Systems Design

Educational Design, and so on" (Banathy, 1984. p. 1-4).

> "Jones noted that there are as many definitions of design as there are those who write about it" (Banathy, 1984, p. 1-1).

Perhaps this uncontrolled variety in design definitions occurs because the individual authors remain unsure of design as design. In this, these authors mirror the difficulties of the creativity authorities. Perhaps Gasparski is correct when he suggests that we need a single definition applicable to a generalized understanding of Design irrespective of the particular product or process of design (1984)?

Applying the guidance of Formal Logic introduced in Section One, we may even venture to say that most of these purported definitions fail to resemble authentic definitions at all. For, they appear to be more like generalized descriptions of particular aspects of design - however design may be ultimately regarded. Professor Banathy (1984. p. 1-2) tells us that:

> Design may be defined as a disciplined inquiry aimed to conceive the idea for a proposed system and to prepare a description of it" (Banathy, 1979).

With this statement, Professor Banathy aptly informs us, at least implicitly, that design signifies a human activity termed disciplined inquiry, and that such an inquiry is a systems-based attempt to provide at least a description, rather than a definition, of a conceived idea. Here we have forthright language conveying the authentic state of understanding of design. Design is something requiring a systems perspective which leads to a description of a conceived idea.

By these few lines, Banathy touches upon the heart of the matter and clearly expresses the dual converging notions that design is a human activity system and that this system concerns itself with the description of a human conception termed a conceived idea. Here Banathy spares us any further intellectual discomfort by not including the notions of person, process or product. And he graces us with logical simplicity of a correct statement about the problem of design - finally. To adequately understand the implications introduced by Banathy's statement, we need to have a better idea of what is meant by a system in general and a human activity system in particular. After all, we need to know what others are talking about whenever they explain that a definition of design requires a systems perspective (Gasparski, 1984), and that design inquiry proceeds from a human activity system (Banathy, 1984).

1: Definition of Systems

As I travel around the world presenting to audiences on various topics in the Computer, Leadership, and Management Sciences, I always makes it a point to ask each audience the following important question:

What is a system?

Unfortunately, I forever receive responses that rank among the most surprising of my professional life:

"A system is **when** you have inputs, processing and outputs".

We already know that you cannot define anything by starting with when. For example, a person or any other Being is not a when, and it cannot be defined as a when. If you know about systems, you will quickly recognize at least three critical problems with this "most very typical" response. In the first place a system consists of at least:

- Input
- Transformation
- Output
- Feedback and Adjustment.

The old and traditional model of input, processing and output expresses the Reductionistic view of a function of a system, or a system's operation, rather than the system itself. The system, to be a system, consists of input and output, like the traditional model, transformation rather than only processing, and very importantly feedback and adjustment processes. As was mentioned in Section One, without Feedback and Adjustment, and most especially Transformation, one never has a system. One may have a procedure. One may have a process. One may have a component of a system. Nevertheless, one does not have a system. A system is all about Transformation. Interestingly, feedback and adjustment, as operations of Systems Science, are invariably missed as part of any response to my question to the audience. Even Harman and Rheingold's work (1984) touched upon in Section One viewed systems under the traditional, and old, Information Theory Model of input, processing and output.

The second disappointment with this answer lies in the fact that the audience typically consists of "seasoned systems professionals" from the world of computer technology and the various levels of corporate business management. These attendees represent an eclectic selection of some of the best personnel within their organizations. Moreover, their organizations trust these attendees with some of the most critical or vital responsibilities that modern Global Corporations possess. Typically, my audiences consist of a large range of:

- Computer Programmers,
- Systems Analysts,
- Systems Designers,
- Systems Managers,
- Management Information Systems Executives,
- Strategic Management Executives,
- Computer Software Development Project Managers,
- Computer Systems Technical Specialists,
- Information Systems Directors,
- Data Management Department Heads,
- Vice Presidents of Systems,
- Corporate Strategic Planning Directors,
- Chief Executive Officers,
- Chief Operating Officers,
- Chief Financial Officers,

- Vice Presidents of Human Resources,
- Members of the Board of Directors.

It is worth noting that the disappointment springs from the fact that such distinguished persons fail to consider the importance of not only Feedback and Adjustment, and especially Transformation, in any system and indeed failed to know about systems at even the most basic and fundamental level. Out of the countless times I asked my question, and regardless of the level of expertise of the attendee, I have yet to receive a proper response. This is a certainly a mind-blowing state-of-affairs. You must remember, these people were the systems professionals of their organizations. They were the people charged with the care and maintenance of their organization's most vital Information and Knowledge-Based Systems and system's resources. No wonder, Computer Software Development has such a terrible performance record. The world is full of people who work hard at actively disappointing their organizations. Such disappointment does not occur by accident. Indifference is more common than one would ever guess. Imagine., developing systems without even knowing what systems are. It is a wonder that we do as well as we do. Previously, in an earlier paper (Newkirk, 1989), I discussed the performance record of computer systems software development accordingly. We all know the horror stories about the countless systems development projects which have remained 90 percent complete for 1000 percent of the time, never to be fully finished at all. In 1979, the Comptroller General of the United States in a Report to Congress, compiled some amazing figures on the success of software projects contracted for the Government.

> These figures indicated that only about two percent of the government's contracted software products worked on delivery, an additional three prevent worked only after some reworking, more than 45 percent were delivered but never

> successful, another 20 percent were implemented but had to be extensively reworked or abandoned altogether, the final 30 percent were paid for but never delivered.

WOW and double WOW! If we tilt this Report in the direction of the business community, we can begin to see how much financial waste and management irresponsibility actually exist in the software development community. For example, one corporation supporting nine software projects constrained by a $6.8 million budget within a cross section of organizations yielded the following results: $.12 million for software that could be used as delivered; $.20 million for software that could be used after changes; $1.30 million for software that was used but had to be extensively reworked or later abandoned; $3.20 million for software that was delivered but never successfully used; $1.98 million for software that was paid for but not delivered. At a cost of $6.8 million, the company received a return on investment, for software development dollars, of a mere $320,000 - about five percent. Large systems projects exceeding the $2 million budget level performed even worse (pp. 4-6).

Obviously, these are shocking figures. They are not recent. However, my experience, and that of others on the staff of various consulting firms I know, indicates that today things are, if anything, probably even worse. Software Development failures and project abandonments remain as common as apple pie. Without attempting to shock anyone, I strongly suggest that the time is past due for such conditions to change:

> "Today, the General Theory of Systems should be the platform of a new beginning for any serious software developer pursuing the production of a new software development methodology appropriate to the dynamic and global problems of today's complex management

> environments and computerized communications networks" (Newkirk, 1979, p. 32). So, I continue to ask those who should know: what is a system?

Finally, the third disappointment which bites me on the leg is the apparent difficulty that people have in responding to my question in the first place. To suggest a definition which begins with "when" or "I feel" rather than "I think" merely serves to offer only a bit of no-knowledge, which is no definition at all. The obvious confusion about the form and substance of definition formulation merely serves to keep the dark veil of ignorance over some very pressing problems, problems which call for the formulation of relevant and appropriate definitions. Apparently, many people have little idea of what it means to define a term or concept, but they do it anyway. At least they make an effort.

I, fully realizing the difficulty of defining a term or concept, for definitions define classes of beings, fully understands the inherent difficulty of my apparently simplistic question: what is a system? In this respect, then, I remain, nevertheless, proud of my audiences for even attempting to respond with a definition, especially sense the task is actually so formidable. Accordingly, I encourage future attempts at rendering a universally acceptable definition for the question, "What is a System?" by suggesting not a definition of a system but a description. After all, people generally describe something when they think they are actually defining something. The give descriptions for definitions. In an effort to close the lop a bit, the approach leading to the following description sprang from an earlier work (Newkirk, 1988) and aptly lays the foundation for a description of a system.

Description of a System

A system is a conceptual being existing in the intentional order of reality, the reality of the mind. Hence, systems exist as logical beings. As such, a system is a contrived structure derived from living and nonliving, i.e., organic and inorganic, subjects consisting of entities, i.e., components or subsystems, connected by a network of interdependent interrelationships. The network is controlled and maintained by feedback and adjustment loops, through mechanisms of command, communications, control, and cooperation, in such a way that the whole system structure, the expansion of the component entities through a proactive process of dynamic equilibrium, manifests behavior marked by a motion towards a particular goal(s) or purpose(s), which is its organizing principle and which energizes the system into action.

Moreover, the interdependence of the components, which are changed by being in the system and changes the system by being in it, and which would alter the system's performance if any component leaves it, forms a hierarchy in such a way that an entire single structure emerges as a whole entity containing properties not contained in any of the aggregate components either individually or collectively, as when H20 becomes water. This hierarchy of components forms a set of systems known as a multisystem of peer systems existing in a larger Suprasystem. These peer systems exist in relationships to each other which are recognized as either hierarchical, centralized, or equalitarian. Additionally, the properties contained in the whole entity come-to-be as a result of the process of emergence, a process which separates the behavior of systems apart from that of nonsystems. All system's properties are enlivened by, at least, the four principal classes of systems activates of input, transformation, output, and feedback and adjustment, through the 19 subsystems dedicated to the processing of information, matter-energy, and Matter-Energy¬Information, the degree of activity being regulated by the openness or closeness of the system (Newkirk, 1988, Banathy, 1973, Miller, 1978, Mayon-White & Morris, 1982, Collen, 1987, Checkland, 1981, Hickey, 1971, Copleston, 1962, Ackoff & Emery, 1972)

The above description certainly suggests a mouthful of philosophical insight. Perhaps this may be the reason why so many people have such a difficult time when trying to answer the author's question? Perhaps it may be the reason why so many people do not yet know what a system is? The concept of systems began to take form in the earliest philosophy of the Ancient Greeks. Aristotle touched upon the fundamentals of systems in his theories of Act and Potency and Hylomorphism (Newkirk, 1972). Many authorities in Informatics still regard systems as entities consisting of input, processing and output. As we have seen, such a view is not quite right and has more to do with the functions of a system's component rather than with the whole system itself. The entire system is more represented by the aspects termed input, transformation, output and feedback and adjustment. Hence, the Informatics authorities do not go far enough in their explanation of systems.

Aristotle, in his Doctrine of Hylomorphism, (Hickey, 1971, Newkirk, 1972) explained that two beings termed Primary Matter and Substantial Form enter into a Potentiality, i.e., a possible relationship as when the soul, the substantial form, and the matter, primary matter, of a man come together as inputs in a relationship, to form the human man, the signate matter. Moreover, as these inputs of substantial form and primary matter enter into "Relationship" they become something totally different, i.e. transformation, as they emerge from the transformation as a human person, something they were not in themselves as primary matter and substantial form alone. The whole process is mediated through feedback and adjustment by the essence of the primary matter and substantial form which act as the essential nodes of the emerging whole being termed human person. Through

Hylomorphism, an act occurs because a potency for such an act pre-existed. Hence, taking a cue from Aristotle, we can say that human beings come to be as the result of a Hylomorphic System through the system's aspects of input, transformation, output, and feedback and adjustment. Apparently, the concepts of systems and systems aspects have been around for more than two thousand years.

What we do today is take such original ideas as those of Aristotle's, and other's as well, and break them down into their basic components. The idea here is to obtain a degree of clarity more comfortable to the contemporary mind which does not seem so drawn to such metaphysical thinking. After all, through the intervening centuries since The Philosopher, many intellectual movements occurred which provided a new paradigm for viewing human earthly life. Section One touched upon this phenomenon.

Ackoff presented a worthy summary of this historical motion in the first chapter of his work *Creating the Corporate Future* (1981, pp. 6¬24). In light of the foregoing, then, when the above description, my description, is given at least a cursory examination, we see that the description basically contains only four segments. These segments conform to the model of Mayon-White & Morris:

1. A system is an assembly of components connected to an interdependent interrelationship in an organized way.
2. The organized assembly of components does something. From this interaction, the system strives to be Purposeful and have function.
3. The components are affected by being in the system and the behavior of the system is changed if they leave it. From this interaction, the system strives for:

- Integrity,
- Coherence,

- Integrity.

The observer of the system, as being of some particular interest, may formally interact with the system and thus change it. From this interaction, the system strives to have value and meaning (1982). From an analysis of the preceding systems descriptions, along with the definition provided by Mayon-White and Morris, we see that systems are multi-structural, meaning, that they can fit anywhere on a continuum from:

- Simple to Complex,
- Open to Closed,
- Mechanistic to Dynamic, and so forth (Banathy, 1984).

4. The assembly has been identified by a least one.

The systems of traditional science, those highlighted by reductionistic experimentation often reflect the more restricted, mechanistic, closed dimensions of systems. However, the systems marked by the problems of contemporary human earthly life, such as the problems of organizational management and those more representative of the ever emerging "systems paradigm", contain systemic, pluralistic, complex and open dimensions. These systems differ somewhat from the traditional view of systems as hard, physical entities existing in the world of reality such as a nuclear reactor, computer, and so forth. But all systems derive from the experience and perception, and even purpose, of an observer.

We only view a nuclear reactor as a system because we first make it so in the intentional order of reality, the reality of the mind. Many persons quickly forget this fact about systems and confuse the hard systems of engineering science such as nuclear reactors as fundamentally something more real than the soft systems of organizations. In some instances, the inputs may differ, and the measurement of such inputs suggest different problems, but each system derives from the intentional order of reality. After all, the nuclear reactor, the "hard" system, may be real enough but the view of it as a system is an intellectual view. It has been the author's experience that the "soft" systems of organizations, human activity systems, have been the more ignored of the two. But "soft" systems are no less real, and both are conceptual beings. Hard systems are often less difficult to measure or define. The systems that the author concerns himself most with here in this paper are the open, dynamic systems which include human activity systems.

My experience suggests that closed systems do exist. But they exist only for a short time, the time immediately preceding the death of the system. In the author's mind, closed systems exist as stressed systems, or sick systems, and are most often associated with a mess or failure. If one examines the boundaries of any system to determine the system's degree of health or vitality of that system. I have had success doing so for years.

Now we have some idea of what we mean when we speak of systems. We know that they have four primary aspects, not three as traditionally thought. And we know that systems come in many types existing along an openness or closedness, one may well determine the continuum of dimensions that make them hard or soft. Moreover, we know that if a system becomes a closed system, it becomes a troubled system. So now some of us know more about systems than we did a few moments ago. But to really understand systems, we need to know about Human Activity Systems.

Description of Human Activity Systems

While the broad description of systems given above spoke to a definition of systems in general, the following description will speak specifically to human activity systems. Proceeding from Banathy (1984), we see that:

> The concept of human activity systems is crucially different from that of natural and engineered systems. These latter, once manifested, cannot be other than what they are. Human activity systems, on the other hand, are manifested through the perceptions of human beings who are free to attribute a variety of meanings to what they perceive (Banathy, 1984, p. 1-4).

Thus, a Human Activity System exists as an open system, i.e., a system not fully closed from its environment by its boundaries (Banathy, 1973), in which the aggregate entities forming the system components are human beings who interact within a functional process infrastructure, which meets the general definition of systems, to achieve a specific purpose(s). All previously identified systems aspects, i.e., input, transformation, output, and feedback and adjustment, are contained in human activity systems just as any other system. Hence, borrowing from the existential view of Sartre (Barnes, 1956), the author views a human activity system as a social system contrived by an observer because of a particular interest or value (Mayon-White & Morris, 1982).

The observer maintains such values according to the influencing factors flowing from the observer's weltanschauung, which has agency to define the system, out of a transphenomenal field (Sartre, 1943). Such a field informs the suprasystem containing the contrived system as a component system, or acts as the background of the all-encompassing field which surrounds, engulfs, and contains the numerous and complex relationships of human beings. This includes those relationships which engage in the fundamental systems activities of input, transformation, output, and feedback and adjustment as an energized Human Activity System.

Thus, where Sartre viewed the transphenomenal field, for Sartre the transphenomenality of the self, as that background in which human existence persists, the author employs the term to express that environment in which a human activity system persists, an environment which is ever expanding and contracting. In this sense, then, the author submits that the human activity system exists as a contrived system composed of human agents, or actors, performing the functions of input, transformation, information interchange, output, and feedback and adjustment to achieve specific goals or purposes (Newkirk, 1988). This view gathers substance from the insights of other authorities as well. Checkland (1981) suggests that the particular Weltanschauungen validates any account of a human activity system, while Ackoff and Emery (1972) focus on the importance of purpose in the human system:

> ...a purposeful system whose members are purposeful individuals who intentionally co-produce a common objective and, at a more complex level, an organization with a functional division of labor relative to its common objective(s)" (Banathy, 1984, p. 1-5).

The refinement of the systems description to account for human activity systems is crucial to our discussion of creativity as design. After all, the author has already stated that human beings do design, and if they do it correctly, they do it from the systems perspective. This means that systems thinking energizes the activities that ultimately produce a final design product, the activities already identified as the four principal aspects of systems, input, transformation, output, and feedback and adjustment. An understanding of this final point leads us to see why design must be considered in terms of design systems and the spaces of design. After all, if we claim to be systems thinker, we must realize that a system consists of many component systems termed subsystems. And the author makes no exception for design.

Since design is a system - for it contains the aspects of input, transformation, output, and feedback and adjustment, contains purpose or goals relative to the observer's weltanschauung, exists as a result of the interagency of an observer which defines and controls the boundaries, and experiences the effects of emergent properties - design consists of component systems termed the systems of design. Moreover, in relation to the concept of a"transphenomenal field" borrowed from Sartre, the systems of design exist in related fields termed the spaces of design. The computer software development human activity system, herein termed the Development Group, will serve as a model to describe design in terms of its spaces, systems and activities.

2: Software Development Human Activity System

The Computer Software Development Human Activity System, the Development Group, exists as an open, sociotechnical human activity system. The Development Group is chartered by a formal agency empowered by a larger human activity system possessing the power to delegate such a mandate. Proceeding from such authority, the charter comes into existence as a result of certain specialized needs, requirements or goals existing in the mind of the chartering agency. Moreover, these goals lead to certain specialized functions which require specialized components to perform these functions.

When the components are produced and integrated to form the Development Group, they perform the primary systems functions of input, transformation, output, and feedback and adjustment. The performance of these four basic functions by the Development Group's components, consisting primarily of human beings, directly lead to the attainment of the Development Group's goals, i.e., the satisfaction of the user's or client's needs - which should be the production of a computer software product or problem solution.

However, the Development Group does not energize these four principal systems aspects in a vacuum; for the development Group exists as a peer subsystem or component of a larger suprasystem, which serves as the development Group's environment. Moreover, not only does the Development Group require an environment in which to exist, the transphenomenality of the self-derived from Sartre, and which to receive all of its inputs in the form of matter, information, and energy, but the Development Group requires a formal structure as well.

Fortunately, it receives such structure through the integration, control and adjustment, and maintenance of the Development Group's various member components, its peer subsystems.

To meet the needs of integration, control and adjustment, and maintenance, the Development Group becomes a network of 19 critical and concurrent component systems identified by Living Systems Theory (Miller, 1978) and examined through Living Systems Process Analysis (Collen, 1987). From the foregoing, then, we are able to understand the Development Group as a complex system which consists of environmental relationships, structural form, and processes of operations, or behavior. Banathy (1973) employs a "Systems Models Approach" to examine the:

- Environmental
- Structural, and
- Behavioral dimensions of systems.

Using Banathy's approach (1973), a Systems Models Approach, the Development Group's environmental relationships can be described with an environmental model, its structure with a structural model, the still picture model, and its behavior with a behavioral or process model, referred to as the motion-picture model. Moreover, with the added intervention of Living Systems Theory (Miller, 1978), all three systems dimensions can be further described in terms of organizational effectiveness employing Living Systems Process Analysis (Collen, 1987). Through the interaction and integration of the development Group's component systems, design is carried out and, hopefully, a design product emerges. Hence, design participates in the producer-product relationship, which is, by the way, what the creativity authorities mean by creativity. We have only just begun to examine design and already we see that a vast field of similarities exists between creativity and design.

Toward An Understanding of Design

The Computer Software Development Human Activity System represents an excellent subject for examining design. After all, a primary function of the Development Group centers on the production - the person, process and product - of a new software design or the redesign of an existing software system. Therefore, because of such a strong connection with design, the author will use the Development Group as a subject for examining design in more detail.

In the examination that follows, the author will examine the Development Group by employing an integrated approach using the Systems Models approach developed by Banathy (1973) and Living Systems Theory presented by Miller (1978). The author will examine the Development Group in terms of its current Environmental, Structural and Behavioral Models, and express how these models should be adjusted to conform to the insights of Living Systems Theory. Accordingly, the examination will focus on the Development Group's design component and a new design for the design component and ultimately the Development Group itself. After all, any change to a component of a system represents a change to the whole system itself. The objectives of this examination remain multidimensional and include:

1. A deeper examination of design as creativity and a more comprehensive understanding of Living Systems Theory and its application to design using the Development Group as a model;

1. An analysis of the Development Group according to the concepts and principles of Living Systems Theory with a focus on the Development Group's design component;

1. The presentation of a basic model of the Development Group according to Banathy's Systems Models approach and the Living Systems Theory architecture with a particular focus on the systems of design and the spaces of design;

1. The presentation of a Development Group design component generic model identifying what subsystems are required to make the Development Group more viable, and thus effective, according to Living Systems Theory and the Systems Models approach.

The Design Methodology Paradox

I selected the Computer Software Development Human Activity System, herein referred to as the Development Group, and everything encompassed by it, as a foundation for examining design. Hopefully, such an examination will eventually lead to a detailed description of the Development Group. This description should go well beyond anything that has been presented about the development Group so far in this book. Accordingly, I submit that the Systems Approach remains an essential ingredient in any method of systems description employed to describe the Development Group, especially to the application of the method of systems description outlined by Mayon-White and Morris (1982), and Checkland (1981).

The Software Development Group consists of many complex subsystems which do not adequately support the demands of current computer software design practices. The author holds that current computer software design practices are ideological, meaning that they are attempts at maintaining asymmetrical relations of power (Sampson, 1983). They are ideological in that current software design practices employ methodologies derived principally from the reductionistic methods of the hard science disciplines of the traditional engineering and/or operations management sciences as a means of perpetuating their own legacy rather than designing effective software (Newkirk, 1988).

Subsequently, many of the authentic systems-based design approaches remain ignored. If we remember that the current software development environment is chartered, in most cases, to solve soft systems software problems or to support a fuzzy thinking environment, the paradox becomes clear. We are attempting to design and develop software systems without an appropriate systems-based methodology - after all, the methodologies employed by the hard science engineering disciplines are anything but systems based. For such methodologies produce greater levels of functional decomposition without ever adequately encountering the design environment. Previously, I expressed the paradox thusly:

In this sense, then, I view the computer thinking discipline requiring approaches and methods more appropriate to the type of activity it really is. Associated with this is the concern that traditional methodologies of software development focus so much on the technical tasks of software product development that they overlook the fact that software development is done by human beings, with human beings and for human beings - that the software development group is indeed a Human Activity System (Newkirk, 1988, p. 7).

As can be guessed, the paradox spoken of above erupts from a methodological conflict. While soft systems methodologies are more appropriate for today's complex and dynamic software design challenges, hard science methodologies remain the ones of choice. At this very moment, as I write this book, over 72 different hard science-based methodologies are being actively employed by computer software development "systems" designers in the design of Artificial Intelligence Systems and more robust real-time soft systems or problem solutions. Some of these methodologies include the following:

software development process fundamentally as a soft system.

1. Active and Passive Component Modelling - ACM/PCM;

2. Activity Modelling/Behavior Modelling - A/BM;

3. AXIAL/IBM;

4. Computer Aided Design and Evaluation Systems CADES;

5. Conceptual Information Analysis Methodology - CIAM;

6. Controlled Requirements Expression - CORE;

7. DAta oriented DEsign - DADES;

8. Design of Data Sharing Systems - D2S2;

9. Data Structured Systems Analysis and Design - DSSAD;

10. Data Structured Systems Development - DSSD;

11. Evolutionary Design Methodology - EDM;

12. Entity, Relationship, Attribute, Event - ERAE;

13. Fagan Inspection Methodology - FIM;

14. General Evolutionary Systems Technique and Large Topology - GESTALT;

15. Grammatical Applications Method for Modelling Applications - GAMMA;

16. Gradual Evolution of Information Systems - GEIS;

17. Hierarchical Development Methodology - HDM;

18. Higher Order Software - HOS;

19. Higher Order Software the Rigorous Approach HOSRA;

20. Adaptation of IBM Federal Systems Division Software Engineering Practices - IBMFSD-SEP;

21. Information Engineering Specification Method - IESM;

22. Information Systems Work and Analysis of Changes -ISAC;

23. Information Engineering Methodology - IEM;

24. INFOrmation LOGic - INFOLOG;

25. Inscribed High Level Petri Nets - IML

26. Interactive Design Approach - IDA;

27. Jackson System Development - JSD;

28. Jackson Structured Development - JSD;

29. Jackson Structured Programming - JSP;

30. LBMS System Development Method - LSDM;

31. Method/1;

32. Modular Approach to Software, Construction, Operation and Test - MASCOT;

33. Methodological Engineering with Reduced Instruction Set Elements - MERISE;

34. Nijssen's Information Analysis Method - NIAM;

35. Phase Development Process - PDP;

36. Problem Statement Language/Problem Statement Analyzer - PSL/PSA;

37. PRojektAbwicklungs und DOkumentationsSystem PRADOS;

38. PROMOD;

39. Problem STatement Language/Problem Statement Analyser - PSL/PSA;

40. Rapid Evolution Methodology of Routine Applications - REMORA;

41. Structured Analysis and Design Technique - SADT;

42. System ARchitecture's Apprentice - SARA;

43. System Definition Language - SDL; 44. System Developer - SD;

45. Software Development System - DSD;

46. Structured Analysis and Structured Design - SA-SD;

47. Systems Development Methodology - SDM;

48. Systems Documentation - SYSDOC;

49. Systems Programming Evolution and Checking - SPECK;

50. Software Engineering Procedures Notebook - SEPN;

51. Software Requirements Engineering Methodology - SREM;

52. Structured Systems Analysis - SSA;

53. STRuctured Analysis, Design and Implementation of Information Systems - STRADIS;

54. User Software Engineering - USE;

55. Yourdon;

56. Vienna Development Method - VDM;

57. Warnier-Orr Conventions - WOC;

58. WELLMADE;

59.Function Point Analysis/Link Development Methodology - FPA/ LDM;

60. Core Development Phases Development Methodology of A/I (AI-DLC)

61. Natural Language Programming – NLP

62. Artificial Intelligence Systems Development

This list presents only a representative selection of the available software development methodologies in use today. A simple cursory analysis reveals that they share many common attributes. The evidence strongly suggests that they boiled up from the same technical stew, the ideological mind-set of an industrial age with an engineering preoccupation. Indeed, if we would randomly select a dozen or so software design methodologies, each from a given time frame, and list their Phases, the redundancy would clearly reveal their shared legacy. For example:

1. 1960 - Optner's Five Phase System

    1. Analysis of current live system

    2. Conceptualization of Model (unidimensional)

    3. Model Test Phase

    4. Pilot installation of tested model system
    5. Full installation of model system

2. 1962 - Ellis's Seven Phase System
    1. Definition of mission objectives
    2. Development of mission design
    3. Requirements Analysis Phase
    4. Specifications Phase
    5. Analyze full range of capabilities
    6. Compare Design of mission system
    7. Detailed Structured Design

3. 1968 - Traditional Eight Phase System
    1. Developments/Refinements Phase of Information Requirements Analysis
    2. Development of full range of systems concepts
    3. Approval/Verification
    4. Detail Design Phase
    5. Testing Phase
    6. Implementation Phase
    7. Project Documentation Phase
    8. Review and Evaluation Phase

4. 1969 - Fisher's Seven Phase System

    1. Problem Identification Phase
    2. Problem Description Phase
    3. System Solution Phase
    4. System Programming Phase
    5. System implementation Phase
    6. System Support Function Phase
    7. Detailed Structured Design Phase

5. 1974 - Stein's Eight Phase System

    1. Planning Phase
    2. Architecture Phase
    3. Specifications Phase
    4. Design Phase
    5. Implementation Phase
    6. Integration Phase
    7. Maintenance Phase
    8. Withdrawal Phase

6. 1978 - Orr's DSSD/Development Cycle

    1. Logical Planning
    2. Physical Planning

   3. Logical Requirements Definition
   4. Physical Requirements Definition
   5. logical Design
   6. Physical design
   7. Build
   8. Unit Test
   9. Integration Test
   10. Training
   11. System Installation
   12. Conversion
   13. Acceptance Test

7. 1983 - Jackson's System Development Cycle
   1. The entity action step
   2. The entity structure step
   3. The initial model step
   4. The function step
   5. System timing step
   6. Implementation step

8. 1983 - Birrell & Ould's System Development Cycle
   1. Project Inception Phase

    2. System Definition Phase
    3. System Design Phase
    4. System Production Phase
    5. System Acceptance Phase
    6. Post-Acceptance Development Phase
    7. Project Debriefing Phase

9. 1984 - Newkirk's Structured Gestalt Process

    1. Logical Planning
    2. Physical Planning
    3. Logical Architecture
    4. Physical Architecture
    5. Logical Specifications
    6. Physical Specifications
    7. Logical Design
    8. Physical Design
    9. Integration
    10. Implementation

10. 1986 - Lantz's Prototyping Methodology

    1. determine Feasibility
    2. Study present system

3. Define prototype
4. Build prototype
5. Exercise prototype
6. Convert
7. Install

11. 1988 - Roetzheim's Structured Phased Project

1. Analysis and evaluation stage
2. Marketing stage
3. Design stage
4. Code stage
5. Test and deliver stage
6. Post completion analysis stage
7. Maintenance stage

12. 1988 - Wallace & Company's Unified Methodology

1. Model system requirements
2. Specifications development
3. Develop architectural level design
4. Employ prototyping

13. 1988 - Olle & Company's CRIS Methodoloqy

1. Information Systems Planning

2. Business Analysis

3. System Design

4. Construction Design

An inspection of the preceding 13 software design and development methodologies reveals a lot of the "same old stuff"; only the names and event ordering of the phases have been changed to offer the hope of something new and different. Look at the third methodology of the group, the Traditional Eight Phase System. Phase number seven is dedicated to documenting the system already designed and tested during the previous six phases. Really now, isn't it just a wee bit late to be thinking about documentation for the first time? If one has not documented the system by now, how can one even hope to have a system at all?

Such is the legacy of Reductionism which led so many to think of software design as a discrete activity resulting from the rigorous application of "functional" decomposition, an activity which reduced a system's requirements down to ever lower levels of detail without adequately encountering the environment. The basic presupposition had it that the scientific approach appeared to benefit everything else, surely it would likewise benefit software design. And so reductionism became accepted as the primary approach to software design. Hence, software systems were really never designed using a systems perspective; they were reduced into existence through the eager application of the scientific paradigm.

Remember this:

For a methodology to be valid,

it must be appropriate to its subject.

3: The Great Contributors

Many in the field of software design never questioned the possibility that a reductionistic based methodology, in tune to the traditional scientific method, was inappropriate to the application of systems-based design problems. It is little wonder, therefore, that the record of success in software development remains so poor. Moreover, when we look to the horizon, the situation does not appear to be improving all that much.

The last decade of design witnessed what experts refer to as the "structured revolution". Structure was advocated for everything structured analysis, structured design, and even structured programming. This decade saw software design research and development produce many of the popular structured development methodologies mentioned above. Ken Orr produced his "Output-Oriented Approach" and immediately many supporters touted it as the long sought after panacea which will greatly simplify the software development process by making software design a discipline in its own right. I really appreciated Ken Orr's development approach. He was really an interesting person.

Then there was the structured top-down approach of Philip C. Semprevive, and then the process-oriented approach of:

Larry Constantine,

Tom deMarco

Dorr Dawson

Ed Yourdon,

C. J. Meyers,

H. Katzan,

III.

III was his name. He changed his name from what it was to III. He was one of my favorite people in software systems development. I still remember the first day I met him.

Then there was the Behavior Modelling approach of Greenspand et all. Additionally, the work of E.W. Dijkstra and Warnier influenced many other researchers and ultimately led to many other approaches to Structured Design.

Obviously, many of these software systems development specialists could see their dream of producing a genuinely scientifically based methodology of software development coming closer to realization than ever before. But, should such a dream as that have been the true dream of software designers? Should not they have been more concerned with the development of a systems-based design approach? After all, were they not in the business of designing software Systems, rather than mere functions?

In retrospect, some designers are beginning to understand that the efforts of these specialists, although noble they were, went a long way toward spreading the hard systems engineering ideology of a previous age. In an interesting kind of way, all 72 or so software design approaches listed above evolved from a common experience. Moreover, they continue to share a common paradigm, the Reductionistic, hard systems engineering approach to problem solving and product development, an approach that erupted from the fires of the industrial revolution and covered the progress of future generations.

The repercussions are still being felt in boardrooms all over the world. But these repercussions are insufficient in themselves to force the adoption of a new paradigm. Perhaps Gasparski's statement sums up the situation quite well: "This is the main bone of contention between a modern and the traditional concept of Design, because what we dispute here is a paradigm" (Gasparski, 1984, p. 3). As I previously expressed it in an earlier work:

Indeed, as we see past R&D developments now, the next decade, the last of this century, looks even more promising for those who wish to prolong such ideological traditions in the software engineering discipline. Sadly, for others, those seeking a genuinely systems oriented, systems-based approach to Software Engineering and Software Product Development, the next decade looks even less promising. As I see the trend towards current Artificial Intelligence developments now, a trend for an authentic systems approach to Artificial Intelligence Systems software engineering and a methodological platform upon which to support it, for those of us who are interested in developing an authentic Systems Thinking Approach, the future looks bleak. It looks like an up-hill battle on a war encrusted field well worn by the conflict of Reductionism versus Expansionism. Obviously, the two critical questions that should be driving all software R&D efforts, including the efforts to develop a manageable Artificial Intelligence environment, still remain to be asked:

> are past and current approaches to software systems development really appropriate to their subjects? Can we still apply traditional hard systems methods to nontraditional soft systems problems, those types of problems that are so representative of current Artificial Intelligence and other Information Systems development projects?

Many in the field remain completely unaware of these questions, and when they do become aware, they appear to miss their significance altogether. How else are we to explain the current wave of blindness in this area? Software systems developers need to devote themselves to a study of systems science before they continue down the well-trodden path to methodological oblivion, by designing software systems as if they were elements of a traditional engineering product (Newkirk, 1989, p. 29).

I once heard a software design senior level manager remark that he very much disliked change. And he lives and works in a field that is marked by a very high degree of change. It is not surprising, then, that the record of this same manager's design group is scarred by:

- Failure
- Cost Overruns
- Missed Schedules
- Inadequate Products
- Wrong Systems
- And so forth.

But then, according to the Report of the Comptroller General presented earlier, so is everyone else's. Unfortunately, such specialists fail in many ways and quite often when they design software. They fail whenever they ignore the Systems Paradigm. They fail every time they neglect to design a design methodology appropriate to a specific system type undergoing design or problem solution. Most of all, they fail whenever they do not approach design as a systems-based activity which behaves under the influence of the spaces of design and other systems of design. Unfortunately, lacking systems perspective, these failures will never quite be seen accurately.

The Systems View

Thus far this paper has echoed the importance of being a Systems Thinker. In the design of computer software, systems thinking is essential. But even more important than this is the need for systems thinking in the design and management of the Development Group itself. For here, the systems approach is even more than fundamentally paramount. In an understanding of human activity systems, a systems view is essential. After all, being a systems thinker is the prerequisite to employing the systems approach as a method of design inquiry. And this means that one must become a systems thinker prior to employing the systems approach, discussed throughout this paper as a method of systems inquiry, to any problem deemed inappropriate to the application of the traditional approaches structured in reductionism.

The Systems Approach is particularly well suited to the complexities of today's dynamic Hi-Tech problems. As a problem-solving approach, it offers a workable transdisciplinary method which bridges the gap between traditional areas of problem-solving and an approach which remains open to the patterns of relationships rather than the individual problem domains of traditional science (Newkirk, 1988, p. 3). An inherent concept of the Systems Approach provides the idea that some problems become solvable only when they are seen in relation to other hierarchical components of a system which, when taken together, give rise to emergent properties not existing as the mere sum of all a system's components. Hence, systems inquiry offers a synthetic inquiry.

Fundamental to the Systems Approach is the understanding that certain properties can be treated scientifically only when such properties are viewed as the components of a hierarchical entity which in turn produces emergent aspects not actually present, but only potentially, in any of the individual system's components. Thus, implicit in the systems approach, as opposed to reductionism, is that primary systems attribute termed component synergism. It is this attribute which leads to the emergence of properties not previously found if in the mere sum of all the components, which is mistakenly expected when the reductionistic paradigm is evoked. Hence, the systems attribute of component synergism is responsible for bringing a potential property into existence by combining previously existing properties and transforming them into a new property not existing before (Newkirk, 1988).

What all of this means to us here is that without a systems view, we can never become genuine designers. We may design things spontaneously - and many of us do. But we will never be adequately prepared to tackle the important design problems of this age. If we continue to ignore systems thinking and plough ahead regardless, the results will be expected: we will merely contribute to the statistics of the Comptroller General and remain part of the problem rather than the solution. Moreover, if we continue to ignore the system paradigm, we will be ill-prepared to model design as a human activity, and thus not understand creativity as design. For we will never become proficient with the Systems Models Approach, an approach that is so vital to our understanding of design.

4: The Systems Models Approach

Argyris and Schon (1978) provide a model of the Human Activity System that is very straightforward:

- The system makes decisions in the name of the entire system;
- The system delegates to individual components the authority to make decision for the entire human activity system;
- The system sets boundaries between itself and its environment.

This description of a Human Activity System is interesting in what it tells us, but disappointing in what it leaves out. But then, Argyris and Schon were probably not intending to provide a complete description of the Human Activity System by these simple three statements. Presenting a description of a Human Activity System can impose a very formidable challenge on just about anyone, a challenge requiring a powerful approach to make such a description possible. Fortunately, such a powerful approach exists in the form of the Systems Models Approach (Banathy, 1973). But regardless of the approach employed to describe any system, six stages have to be worked through to make any description meaningful. These stages are referred to as:

Awareness

Commitment

Detection

Separation

Selection

Description (Mayon-White & Morris, 1982).

Moreover, the sixth stage, Description, consists of, at the least, six component modelling activities:

1. The definition of the systems components;
2. The environment which identifies all the environmental components affecting the selected system;
3. Identification of all inputs to and outputs from the system;
4. The processes of the system including the identification of all the state variables of the system;
5. The identification of all relationships existing between the state variables of the process model, the infrastructure model;
6. The structure of the selected system which identifies all of the structural relationships existing between the system's components. These relationships include the goals, functions and components, i.e., the primary entities of the structural model which lead to the satisfaction of the user requirements.

The Development Group, or Team, exists as a complex human group consisting of numerous levels and dimensions of activity, ranging from the most simple to the most complex. Traditional engineering-based development approaches employ modelling techniques which focus on only one or two dimensions of product specifications such as structure and behavior, and so forth. Such a limited approach to modelling often results in product models insufficient or inappropriate to the system design project, i.e., the product undergoing design and development.

Present approaches to software design modelling focus only on the required processes of the intended system or merely the outputs to be produced by the system. Project management frequently ignores the more important human dimensions of the development project. These dimensions include all the environmental issues existing within the interfaces between the design human activity system and this system's environment and design human activity system with each other. Hence, modelling, to be relevant, must illuminate aspects of the whole project process, including the environment, the process and the structure of the project from a multi-dimensional perspective.

An appropriate software design methodology must include a modelling approach. Accordingly, such a methodology must address, and fully model, all the important aspects of the subject under design, i.e., the software product or solution itself in terms of the:

- Components, processes, and relationships of the systems being designed
- Interfaces between the components of the systems being designed
- Behavior and structure of the system
- The environment in which the Design and Development Group must function
- The environment in which the Systems to be Designed must function
- Any component which emerges at the next higher level of the Human Activity System, the Development Group.

Unfortunately, though, many current design approaches offer a restricted facility for modelling in that they remain confined to producing models of only discrete segments, phases, levels, or cycles of the actual product being designed. Hence, the designer produces outputs from each development phase, because designers often inappropriately think in terms of development phases, which models or represents only limited aspects of the required entire product. These phased product outputs are referred to as deliverables. Hence, commonly used approaches to software design often produce sets of interim deliverables termed: the preliminary system design, the detailed system design, the test plan, the conversion plan, and so forth.

Collectively, these deliverables are intended to model the required system. Ultimately, the hope is held, for it is often only a hope, that this final collection of all phased deliverables will be accepted by the client as the final software system, product, or problem solution. Sadly, this hope demonstrates a lack of understanding of the systems approach in that it unnecessarily commits the error termed by the author as the "Fallacy of the Simple Sum", a fallacy through which the designer views the whole system as the simple sum of all the various parts.

Systems thinking reacts to this weakness in reductionism, the Fallacy of the Simple Sum, by suggesting that, in at least in some cases, i.e., social and management sciences, systems components should be examined in configuration or union with other peer systems of their suprasystem, meaning, with the other components of a system. Thus, the designers should focus on the activities of the "whole set", and all this implies. In this way, as we have seen earlier, the designer designs the entire system as an integrated subject, rather than as a decomposed object. Systems thinkers refer to this approach to design as "holism". Systems thinkers view holism as an approach in the search for knowledge that leads to an understanding of a subject by obtaining an in depth understanding of that subject's "wholeness". But holism is only one side of the system coin, the other being emergence.

Briefly, emergence has it that when interacting in the system, the system's components give rise to distinct properties that clearly do not exist in such a complex form within each isolated component. Hence, through emergence, a synergism occurs which causes a new property to exist that did not previously exist when the system's components remained isolated. "A systems view is required to adequately perceive the emergence of such properties" (Newkirk, 1988, pp. 2-3). Holism and emergence are the twin towers of the system perspective. And model building represents the systems way of viewing an entire problem domain.

5: Systems Approach to Modelling

The systems approach views problems from a broader perspective. While traditional approaches remain firmly grounded in reductionism, the systems approach advocates expansionism. The systems approach produces models that provide a comprehensive view of the environment, structure and behavior of a subject (Banathy, 1973). Thus, while traditional modelling approaches normally limit themselves to a single aspect of an entire problem domain, by ever deepening phases of reductionism, the system approach takes in the entire subject-transphenomenal relationship, meaning, the system and its environment from the observer's own weltanschauung.

Furthermore, while model building in most instances serves as only a tool or technique within the design and development arsenal of traditional software development methodologies, the same cannot be said for the systems approach. For systems thinkers, model building represents an entire way of viewing a problem domain. Hence, for systems thinkers, model building becomes an entire approach in its own right. For the authentic systems thinker, then, modelling becomes the appropriate systems approach, meaning method, for describing systems, i.e., problem domains. While traditional software development views modelling as one aspect of an approach to software design, the systems perspective views modelling as the foundation for the complete design methodology. Hence, for the systems thinker, everything related to modelling, i.e., tools, techniques, approaches, and so forth, becomes a paramount concern in the design of any design methodology. After all, every advance in human progress is first preceded by an advance in methodology. The elevation of the significance of modelling to the design process is another aspect which marks the systems approach and sets it out as something distinct from traditional approaches. "...the product of design is a representation of a future system. Consequently, knowledge about models and model building is a main concern to anyone who studies and practices design" (Banathy, 1984, p. 5-1).

Naturally, reflecting on Professor Banathy's words immediately brings up the question: what is modelling? To quote Professor Banathy once again, we see that: "The term model has several meanings. Underlying all the meanings is the notion that a model is a construct or description that represents or stands for something" (1984, p. 5-1). Models can be deductive or inductive. If deductive, they mirror an already existing system, i.e., physical representation of current system; if inductive, they mirror future or planned systems (Banathy, 1984).

Obviously, inductive models are the ones of most concern to designers. "Design is a representation of a desired future state of a system and that representation is the model of the future system" (Banathy, 1984, p. 5-2). Inductive models exist as solution models whenever they represent a planned system, i.e., Banathy's "something to be made" (1984, p. 5-2). But when inductive models describe how the designer is to conduct design and validate it, these models become design process models (Banathy, 1984, 5-2).

Lippitt (1973) noted that models serve to enhance the designer's perception and express it. Lippitt (1973) also views the skills of the model maker, and thus designer, as related to the characteristics of creative persons. Hence, Lippitt suggests that model makers have to possess: confidence, situational sensitivity, independence of judgment, ability to abstract, mental flexibility, tolerance for ambiguity, and the twin abilities to analyze and synthesize (Banathy, 1984). Apparently, authorities on design think in terms of creativity, while authorities on creativity think in terms of design. But Hanneman (1975) offered a formal definition of the model as a structure of symbols with a set of rules for relating the symbols within that structure. Hanneman sees several disadvantages to models including: overemphasis on form, oversimplification, overemphasis on rigor, and pictorial overcome these disadvantages, Hanneman realism.

To suggests some general criteria to guide our selection of an appropriate process model. Accordingly, the model should reflect:

1. The nature of the process being studied;
2. The level of knowledge currently existing about the design process;
3. The level of measurement that the model requires, versus the level of measurement that can actually be achieved;
4. The desired goal or end product aspired to by the designer including his or her personal level of sophistication in design methods;
5. The resources and time available;
6. The fundamental utility of the model itself (Banathy, 1984, pp. 5-6, 5-7).

From a practical viewpoint, business sector software designers rarely consider Hanneman's third criteria listed above. In the first place, they rarely become concerned about the level of measurement their designs require, and they virtually never think about the level of measurement they can achieve in their design review.

Software designers reserve such concerns for the domain of Quality Assurance and Control; and these domains concern someone else.

From another direction, Odum (1971) viewed model building as a means of expressing through simplification the essential features of complex ecological and social systems. His view expresses the thinking of many systems thinkers.

Bakker (1979), considered models from yet another direction and categorized models into three primary types:

- Preference Models - express the decision maker's goals and values;
- Consequence Models - provide information on what happens if scenarios, i.e., what consequences result in a given environment because of a certain course of action and how will the antagonist react?
- Decision Models - help determine optimal solutions to a problem by acting as abstractions of the decision logic (Banathy, 1984).

Michael Florian (1974) reminds us that we must consistently tailor a model to an eventual use. Accordingly, Floriam proposed that designer answer the following questions for their models:

- Is the model descriptive or normative?
- Is the model static or dynamic?
- Is the model an aggregate or desegregate? 4. What is the precision need for the model?
- In what environment is the model to be implemented?
- How will the end-users interact with the model's input and output?
- What criteria may be used to validate the model (Banathy, 1984).

To summarize what the various authorities have expressed about model making and design, Banathy (1984) vividly points out that model building has some direct implications for design thinking. He states:

> I now propose that there is a certain type of thinking that is characteristic of designers who build models of human activity systems. This type of thinking is different from that

> of scholars in the various disciplines or design professionals in, for example, engineering or architecture (Banathy, 1984, p. 5-11).

Furthermore, Banathy (1984) points out that whenever designers think about the design of human activity systems, they must concern themselves with three important considerations: "goodness of fit", "patterns and context", and "the significance of discontinuity". In regard to the last concern, Banathy continues to say that: "In design, there is often a discontinuous jump from one sort of design insight to the other" (1984, p. 5-14). The author wonders if Banathy's concern here is the same as that expressed by the creativity authorities when they refer to the "sudden insight" of creativity? Here is another place where we might ask: Is not design and creativity really the same?

By now, our minds should be forming a picture of the close bond existing between the design process and modelling. In systems thinking and practice, modelling stands as the kernel of all design activity. Hence, from the systems perspective, whenever the author talks about design, implicitly, he also talks about modelling. After all, modelling is a most rudimentary way of thinking about systems and the design of systems.

Moreover, models covey the individual expression of a perceived system as recognized and designed by an observer. Hence, models signify a descriptive event of an observer. Checkland writes:

> Some very rudimentary systems thinking has been expounded. Such thinking starts with an observer¬describer of the world outside ourselves who for some reason of his own wishes to describe it "holistically", that is to say in terms of the whole entities linked in hierarchies with other wholes. This leads to the most basic prescription of what the

> observer's description will contain: his purpose, the system(s) selected, and various systems properties such as boundaries, inputs and outputs, components, structure, the means by which the system retains its integrity, and the coherency principle which makes it defensible to describe the system as a system (1982, p. 121).

The basic prescription of what the observer's description will contain is a personalized one at best. A fundamental ingredient in any systems description

always rests upon the world view of the observer. The experience, education, beliefs, social structures, habits of the intellect and will, family background, values, likes and dislikes, levels of acculturation, and so forth all come together through the synthesis of a dynamic equilibrium to form the observer's world view, the weltanschauung of the observer. Doubtlessly, since no two people share exactly the same view of the world, it is unlikely that they share exactly the same view of any system, especially those systems defined as soft systems. For obviously, no two people are identical in every respect (Newkirk, 1988).

Recognition of the subjectivity involved in the systems description process makes imperative the need for a balanced approach to systems description. Such an approach should be provided by a methodology designed to defuse any potential weakness in the description process and provide a structure where structure is lacking. For the Development Group, this means that design should proceed only through the auspices of an authentic systems-based methodology, a methodology through which the development Group is best able to resolve problems particular to Soft Systems Thinking while at the same time controlling the subjectivity of the individual design team members who are participating collectively as both systems observers and describers.

Lanyon and Goodstein (1982) tell us that "immediate, organized, and direct" intuition informs an observer's powers of observation more so than learning. But intuition alone remains insufficient to determine an appropriate system- based methodology. Rather such a methodology flows only from an in-depth understanding of the principles of systems thinking. Accordingly, a core outline of a recommended system-based methodology now follows, not from the author's intuition but rather as the outcome of an intellectual evolution, as evolving from more than 27 years in the system field. By the expression, "system-based methodology", the author means:

> A collection of methods, performed and described in a systematic way, that is capable of being taught, scheduled, measured, compared and modified if necessary, and that focuses on the four principal aspects of systems in terms of operations to be performed, i.e., input, transformation, output, and
>
> feedback and adjustment operations (Newkirk, 1988, P, 36).

Any methodology ensuing from the principles contained in the outline characterizes the dynamic relationships stressed above, relationships which can be as expansive and as broad as one's weltanschauung may permit. Moreover, this outline, derived from Checkland (1981) and the Development Group architecture, provides the methodological foundation for conducting a systems description, including the description of a system's behavior, especially the process of systems design.

The Outline of a Systems Based Methodology for Design:

1. The problem situation unstructured - provide a model of the total situation in which a problem is perceived.
2. The problem situation expressed - convert the result of the initial analysis into an unstructured picture revealing "how structure and process relate to each other within the situation" under examination.
3. Name and define all relevant systems by providing a root definition of any system determined to be relevant according to the criteria of usefulness and trial and error.
4. Develop and test conceptual models of the defined relevant systems.
5. Evaluate current conceptual models against the formal systems models.
6. Conduct research on additional systems thinking and apply any findings to the models making them even more relevant and complete.
7. Compare all conceptual models with reality. Four approaches are possible:

- Use the models to perform ordered questioning.
- Make a straight comparison of current reality with the models.
- Create a model of what currently exists and overlay this model with the conceptual model of the root definition produced in step three above. From this determine the root definition of the current what exists model.
- Use the models as a basis for obtaining historical accounts of previous processes and outcomes and then use this information as data to compare the historical results with those derived from the models.

1. Identify and list the results of stage seven above as desirable and feasible changes.

2. Implement feasible and desirable changes.

6: The Formal Systems Model

More often than one would ever imagine, systems research will require a Formal Systems Model as a control mechanism to better enable a designer to more appropriately determine the gap between the reality of what actually exists and what is lacking in the systems model. I refer to this as the Existential Gap between the Systems Capabilities and the Systems Essentialities. This enables systems designers to better determine the difference between what system exists and what system is possible. As Aristotle would tell us: This is the simple difference between systems actuality and systems potentiality or the reality of what exists and what is lacking in several possible worlds. This process of system differentiation enables designers to more formally decide which systems model is the one that teams should implement and what changes should the systems designers make and then implement. As is obvious, formal systems models are important to everybody because they facilitate the process of determining the validity of any systems model and thus determining the conditions that increase the necessity for designing these formal models as a standard that teams can employ for evaluating the depth and degree of completeness of these Formal Systems Models. The more important aspects for using a formal model include:

1. The model includes a continuous, i.e. on-going, purpose or mission - or goals and objectives if it models a hard system.

1. The model includes a measure of performance to indicate that progress is occurring, and everything to do what such progress such as how, where, when, how much, by whom, and so forth.

1. The model contains a mechanism for supporting the decision-taking process.

1. The model contains other models of subsystems which are systems in their own right conforming to the formal systems model and containing all the properties of systems, i.e. aspects of input, transformation, output, feedback and adjustment.

1. The model's components interact in such a way that the system's effects and actions flow through the system.

1. The model exists as a subsystem or component of a wider system in which it exists; hence, it has an environment with which it exchanges inputs and outputs.

1. The model remains separated from its environments by recognizable boundaries. These boundaries enclose a systems domain in which real power environment.
2. The model describes the actual resources, both physical and abstract, which exist under the direction of the decision-taking process.

1. The model describes a system's long-term stability or continued existence - as when the model describes the system's on-going mission or purpose.

The formal model offers the designer a standard against which to keep oneself in line all throughout the design process, from beginning to end, rather than after design completion. In many cases of software systems design, because of the client's ignorance about their own requirements, designers do not know if they are moving in the right direction until after their design has been fully implemented. And then it is often too late to make corrections. In many cases

is exerted on the corrections are usually so severe that a new system has to be designed from the ground floor. In large corporations, such cases of software failure are more common than many would like to admit. Working with the

designers of the future. Indeed, the hope for the future rests in the client's capacity for doing design themselves and this is the hope of the futurists, make no mistake about it. Since design is creativity, the client can become as creative as anyone else. But, nevertheless, in the short run at least, the client's vagueness about what technical assistance they really want and their inability to adequately express their requirements in technical terms to a technical community, and vice versa, presents designers with a significant problem.

The Problem Defined

Throughout the design process, a weakness exists that prevents the various teams from coming altogether. The client, or end-user, requesting the product or software design frequently exists in a self-imposed technical vacuum. Hence, the client remains unaware or unsure of what requirements their genuine system needs. In some cases, the end-user presents the most difficult challenge for the systems designers to the extent that many clients ultimately fail to recognize the importance of the System Model or simply ignore whatever is presented to them by the designers.

Obviously, the end-users may know what they want, but they are incapable of stating their requirements with the necessary amount of detail and in the most appropriate manner. More often than not, however, the end-user only enjoys some vague notion or "gut-feeling" about what kind of system they require for their operations. They simply believe that the require something, some computerized system, and computer software design, and some systems-oriented methodology to adequately deal with their often vague, business directed generalities flowing from the client's fuzzy thinking. Rather, the designers who use such traditional methodologies tend to view all aspects of the end- user's requirements for a new system as they all resulted from the strict definition of a hard systems problem. Hence, the designers perpetuate the ideological myth that the problems associated with the software engineering of fuzzy requirements can be viewed as traditional engineering problems.

> "Ultimately, in many instances, the methodologies become inappropriate to the problems they are employed to solve because they bring hard systems thinking to bear on soft thinking problems" (Newkirk, 1988, p. 24).

Rather than committing to an authentic analysis of the client's fuzzy requirements through appropriate means, common software development practice employs the actual fuzzy feeling of the clients to improve their systems.

The commonly accepted in-house software design methodology still remains the most often used approach to defining the client's fuzzy language and soft systems thinking.

Regardless of the methodology employed, whether the structured procedure driven method of Yourdon or the data driven, output oriented approach of Orr's, by default and misapplication, that methodology becomes a mere client language analysis tool rather than an appropriately matched software development methodology. For, in many organizations, design is conducted as analysis. In view of the preceding, I previously wrote:

> The process of software development becomes subverted by using the development life cycle to define the user's requirements. Following this, the real task of software development normally commences. Unfortunately, the damage has been done. A singular development methodology has been used, not for development but for performing the activities of requirements definition. The product of such a technical misdeed often signifies that a methodology has been employed which was not appropriate to its subject. Hence, it was invalid. Remember, for a methodology to be valid, it must be appropriate to its subject (Newkirk, 1988, p. 26).

The Root Definition

Designers design and analysts analyze. Analysis provides input to design. Design provides a model of the system. If the model represents a future system, it becomes an inductive model. Designing and modelling are two sides of the same coin. How can one produce a model without doing design? How can one produce a design without doing model building? The problem exists when designers do design and call it analysis. When this happens - and it does - projects become unmanageable, and the integrity of the software becomes compromised. Ultimately, the design itself may little resemble the system requested by the client. After all, the client will not know what their system requirements are until the first system is implemented. In this way, every system implemented merely serves to act as an alternative system submitted as a potential client problem solution. And there are much better ways to define alternate systems.

The designers must, and I mean must, be free to build models of alternate designs based upon inputs received from a thorough investigation of the client's demands consisting of repeated cycles of analysis and synthesis using a formal system model. This means that a project infrastructure must be designed to support the system approach to soft systems design. Such a project infrastructure must define the method of analysis as distinct from that of design while identifying the relationship of each to the other as consisting of a peer relationship which has each as peer components in an overall software development system.

Analysis is critical to design in that it provides the verbs upon which all the root definitions of the system are modelled. As we have seen in Section One, definitions are difficult to formulate. The formulation of root definitions offer a method of overcoming the limitations of the classical definition methods

activity rather than classes of being. Hence, root definitions, although not really definitions of any being in the strict sense as when we say that a man is a rational animal, tell us about systems being identifying that systems activities.

The development of a root definition for any Human Activity System, including the design system, consists of two stages that were outlined earlier by identifying types of systems. It is good to remember that the root definition must conform to a Formal Systems Model of Human Activity Systems. Hence, the root definition must embody, as far as is possible, the six essential characteristics of the Formal Root Definition Model, those termed CATWOE:

C - Customer in terms of the user, client, victim, the terminal point or beneficiary affected, or on the receiving end of the systems central activities or outputs;

A-Actor or actors in terms of any agent central to the transformation process of the system; after all, without actors no transformation is possible;

T - Transformation in terms of the main activity of the system. Transformation acts as the nucleus of the Root Definition and is expected to include the direct object of the central activity verb or verbs;

W - Weltanschauung in terms of the world-view

outlook implicit in any root definition imposed spontaneous manner by the giver of the definition;

O- Ownership of the system in terms of control, concern, or sponsorship;

E - Environment and wider system constraints in terms of the interaction and impositions of systems in which or in addition to which the ownership system exists (Checkland, 1981).

7: C-A-T-W-O-E

Formal Systems Models and Root Definitions go hand and hand, just like design and modelling. In the case of the Development Group, a Formal System Model and Root Definition Matrix may be synthesized out of the following definition:

> The computer software development human activity system is a system chartered by a corporation or agency to produce computer software for approved software users in conformance to defined user requirements of product and performance criteria. These criteria are assured by the appropriate human components of the development human activity system as it directs the application of software tools and technologies throughout the course of the product development life cycle according to the disciplines of software engineering, project management and business planning under the constraints of time, cost, technology, and human resources (Newkirk, 1988, p 54).

This definition provides a comprehensive view of the Development Group. Moreover, it lends itself well to the format of the Formal System Model as it contains the following Formal System Model properties:

1. Objectives, Mission or Purpose "to produce computer software for approved users";

2. Measure of Performance - "in conformance to defined user requirements of product and performance criteria";

3. Decision-taking process "These criteria are assured by the appropriate human components";

4. Components - "the appropriate human components of the development human activity system";

5. Connectivity - "as it directs the application of software tools and technologies throughout the course of development";

6. Wider Systems Environment - "is a system chartered by a corporation or an agency";

7. Boundaries - "is a system chartered by a corporation or an agency to produce software for approved software users";

8. Resources - "under the constraints of time, cost, technology, and human resources";

9. Continuity - "is a system chartered by a corporation or agency". This attribute cannot exist as something ephemeral and must speak to realistic longevity. After all, if a system lacks continuity, it can long remain a system - indeed, it cannot be a system at all.

The definition of the Development Group given above sits quite well with the Formal Systems Model, as we have just seen. But we do not rest here, for we must also be sure that the characteristics of the root definition expressed by the mnemonic CATWOE likewise exist as relevant to the nine properties of the Formal System Model, the FSM. Thus, the Root Definition characteristics relevant to the Formal System Model can be expressed accordingly:

1. Customer – "in conformance to defined user requirements";

1. Actors - "the appropriate human components of the development human activity system" and "These criteria are

assured by the appropriate human components";

1. Transformation - "to produce computer software for approved users";

1. Weltanschauung - "to produce computer software for approved users";

1. Owner - "is a system chartered by a corporation agency";

1. Environmental and Wider System Constraints "as it directs the application of software tools and technologies throughout the course of development" ... "under the constraints of time, cost, technology, and human resources".

When we synthesize the characteristics of the Root Definition with the nine properties of the Formal or breakdown structure:

1. Objective, Purpose or Mission - Transformation - "to produce computer software for approved users";

2. Measure of Performance - Customer - "in conformance to defined user requirements";

3. Decision-taking Process - Actor(s)/Owner "These criteria are assured by the appropriate human components" ... "is a system chartered by a corporation or agency";

4. Components - Actors - "the appropriate human components of the development Human Activity System";

5. Connectivity – Environmental and Wider System Constraints" as it directs the application of software tools and technologies throughout the course of development";

6. Wider Systems Environment - Owner - "is a system chartered by a corporation or agency";

7. Boundaries - Environmental and Wider System Constraints and Actor(s) - "is a system chartered by a corporation or agency" and "the appropriate human components of the development human activity system";

8. Resources Environmental and Wider System Constraints "as it directs the application of tools and technologies throughout the course of development" ... "under the constraints of time, cost, technology, and human resources";

9. Continuity - Owner - "is a system chartered by a corporation or agency".

On a more formal note, the finalization of the Root Definition for the Development Group, and the definition's synthesis with a Formal System Model completes the fifth stage in the method of systems description outlined previously. More often than not, root definitions of most systems are found to be inadequate, inappropriate or otherwise incomplete. When this happens, the designer must revisit previous stages in the method of systems description and re-work them. The aim is to produce a root definition which includes most, if not all, of the six characteristics of root definitions just outlined.

Whenever a decision is made to exclude any characteristic from a definition, the rationale for such a decision must be defended and not left to change. in fact, the rationale should always be predetermined. When observing a system, the observer's point-of-view, the observer's specific field of interest, will determine the system's formal root definition. The Development Group, for example, may have many different root definitions depending upon who is doing the defining. And in real practice, this is often the case. No wonder software requirements are so difficult to design Experience has taught us that little difficulty is required to talk about the same system very differently - with very different expectations, attitudes, beliefs, needs, and knowledge. One's root definition of any system depends upon one's weltanschauung. Hence, the author submits that a root definition, to be useful, should be as broad in scope as the responsibility of the observer presenting it.

8: Describing a Human Activity System

While the first five stages in our method to describe the Systems Approach can to some extent be considered as high level preparatory activity, in the sixth stage things change significantly. For here in the sixth stage, we concentrate on delivering a greater depth of detail about our selected system, i.e, for our purposes here, the computer software design human activity system. This detail should become the product of a rigorous and analytical examination of the selected and defined system which is synthesized through a systems-based approach. Hence, all analysis occurs after the observer confronts the system's environment. Subsequently, the rigorous examination, i.e. observation, as was previously pointed out, will include analysis and modelling, i.e. design, of the following:

1. The system's components;
2. The system's inputs;
3. The system's outputs;
4. An environmental model including its primary components;
5. A structural model indicating the relationship existing between the systems components;
6. A process model indicating the state variables of the system and the relationships existing between the model's state variables.

The Systems Components

The Development Group consists of a collection of persons who have joined together under corporate charter to produce computer software systems or programs. In the process, the Development Group may design either applications software, or computer systems software, or even both. To meet the mandate of its charter, the Development Group becomes organized around a formally defined "division-of-labor". In each instant where a division of labor occurs, a component, subsystem, or even a subcomponent of the original system becomes formalized by the definition of boundaries which separate each component from any of the others. This separation occurs in respect of the type of activity performed and the product delivered by each component. The components function in such a way that their activities lead to the emergence of a collective product containing properties not found in any of the products taken individually. Hence, the structure of the system of components can be viewed as hierarchical rather than linear and the final product of the hierarchical structure can be said to be greater or essentially different than the individual products of each component.

Paradoxically, the whole system's structure evolved from a simple top-down functional decomposition of the whole system into its component parts through an analysis of the system's structure-determined functions. Moreover, using the systems perspective of encountering the environment, the whole system's product emerges from a complex bottom-up functional composition of the product of each component into a final product of the whole system. This whole system, consequently, becomes more than the "simple sum" of all component products in that the system's product contains properties not found in any of the previous products if they were merely combined. Hence, the hierarchical emergence of the whole system's component products leads to completely new products not previously found in any component or simple combination of components.

In the case of the Development Group, a few of the components, or subsystems, responsible for the production of software deliverables such as designs, programs, test plans, and so forth, include:

1. Management Components:

    - Systems management
    - Project Management
    - Team or group management

2. Analysis components

3. Design Components

4. Programming Components

5. Testing

6. Technical writers

7. Librarian support groups

8. Technical services support groups:

    - Data Administration
    - Data Base Administration C. Auditors
    - Systems security groups
    - Computer operations groups
    - Quality Assurance and Control

9. User community groups wherever appropriate

The Design Component

As can be seen from the brief outline above, the Development Group consists of several components. Some are technical, while other are administrative. The Design component stands out as one of the most critical technical components of the entire system, the entire Development Group. Since the author has consistently argued throughout this entire paper that creativity is design, he will focus the remainder of this paper on the design component of the Development Group, along with a look at the processes of design and the products of design, already referred to as model. To do this, I will employ the Systems Approach and examine the design using Living System Theory (Miller, 1978) and the Systems Models Approach (Banathy, 1973). To identify and describe the component systems of any living system, including Human Activity System, and how these components respond to a system's matter, energy and information, the Systems Models Approach (Banathy, 1973) concentrates primary on the modelling of the environment, structure and behavior of any system, including the primary systems examined by Living Systems Theory, LST.

With the systems approach, an observer only needs to determine on which system to concentrate. For example, does an observer wish to study the entire Development Group from a holistic perspective, or does (s)he merely wished to study one of the Development Group's subsystems as we are doing here.

When an observer focuses only on one system of the Development Group, regardless of the system, (s)he still needs to think about the system's inputs and outputs, i.e., matter-energy-information, the system's subsystems, and especially the system's environment, structure and behavior. If the system happens to be the design component of the Development Group, this means that the observer must examine all of the above in terms of the systems and spaces of design, the processes of design, the design products, and so forth. Hence, the systems perspective offers a comprehensive understanding of its subject even if the subject exists merely as a single component, or subsystem, of a larger, all -encompassing Suprasystem.

The Environmental Model of Design

In the Development Group, Design exists as both a process and a component. Not without reason, the design component is viewed as the only truly "creative" component of the entire Development Group. This component comes-into-being through the auspices of a formal organizational mandate that says the Design Component will perform software design for the Development Group specifically and the Corporation at large. Hence, the Design System is located within its environment. Hence, in the broad systems view, the Design Component becomes a human activity system, subsystem, of a much larger, parent system termed the suprasystem, i.e., the Development Group. Hence, the suprasystem exists prior to the Design Component.

The Design Component is itself designed to respond to the computer software design needs of a specific client or user organization, internal or external to the corporate suprastructure. These needs often range from the simplest to the most complex. Hence, the organization structure of the Design Component must be such as to permit it to respond quickly, efficiently, and effectively to the diverse demands of the Development Group and indirectly to the client community and the corporate strategic imperative. This means that the Design Component must consists of a number of critical subsystems which perform the activities required of it by the Development Group and permit it to respond correctly to any acceptable client request.

Living Systems Process Analysis (Collen, 1987) examines the critical subsystems of a Human Activity System, and this includes the Development Group's Design Component, and helps determines the rate and range of that system's effectiveness as the system works to meet its purpose, goals or objectives. Hence, the application of Living Systems Process Analysis, LSPA, as we shall see in Section Three, helps an observer provide an additional description of the Design Component's most critical subsystems, numbering 19 in all. By doing so, LSPA seeks to answer the following two questions:

1. Who participates in the subsystem process?

2. What does each person do to make the process happen?

This means that Living Systems Process Analysis concentrates primarily on the "traditionally defined organizational entities and general flows which are involved in carrying out the process" of each critical subsystem (Collen, 1987). The aspect which we are most concerned with here is how the Design Component of the Development Group generally performs its software design duties through the input, throughput, transformation, output, and feedback and adjustment sequence of matter-energy and information (Newkirk, 1989).

The Design Component's suprasystem is that component's environment. Hence, by being the component's environment, the Development Group becomes the context in which the Design Component exists. The Development Group is a complex system in its own right and includes everything which can possibly surround or affect the Design Component, or may be affected by the Design Component. Thus, the environment acts as the multisystem which provides the Design Component with the component's expectations, demands, constraints, requirements, capital resources, personnel, management directives, customers or users, technologies, and so forth, which form the Design Component's actual input stream.

In the specific case of the software design human activity system, the input stream includes software designers, perhaps programmers and systems analysts, computers and facilities, contracts, legal requirements, corporate policies and procedures, consultants, security measures, financial support, schedules, departmental clients and client requests, design methodologies, tools and techniques, which may enter the component from a source external to the Development Group, knowledge, experience, and anything which may help the Design

Component meet the requirements of its charter. In simple terms, inputs collectively include everything the Design Component received from its environment.

As can be seen, then, a specialized part of the corporation, the software engineering discipline environmental subsystem, acts as the Design Component's environment. As such it provides input to the Design Component which permits that component to design computer software in accordance with state-of-the-art knowledge of leading-edge industry wide software design practice. In addition to this very important contribution, the environmental system, the component's suprasystem, provides many other inputs to the component as well.

To perform the four fundamental functions of a system, i.e., input, transformation, output, and feedback and adjustment, and to remain an open system, the Design Component must continually receive inputs from the environment and send outputs to it. Such input/output transfer activity must commence at software design initiation and continue until product acceptance. This means that a continuous stream of inputs and outputs must regularly pass through the component-environment boundary.

Moreover, the component's complexity is such that the input and output flow must pass through the component-environment boundary via the component's component-component and component-environment boundaries, meaning, that inputs and outputs must often proceed from one component of the Development Group to another and then from these components through the component-environment boundary to the appropriately designated client component. For example, the analysis requirements must proceed through a quality assurance and control review component, via a technical walkthrough, prior to their release to the Design Component or the client community for approval. Hence, information transfer between the component and its environment occurs as a complex activity often preceding the transfer of information, or raw data, between the components of the development Group.

Furthermore, in many instances, the input and output passing between the component's boundaries adopt many forms. Indeed, everything received by the Design Component from its environment is termed the component input and everything sent by the Design Component back into the environment is termed the system output (Newkirk, 1987).

Traditional View of Input and Output

From a traditional point-of-view, for the Design Component Human Activity System, the various types of input and output passing through the component- component boundaries and component-environment boundaries may include:

1. Inputs:

- Group charter
- Knowledge of General Systems Theory -Rules and procedures of software design -Human experience
- Previous software documentation -Client requirements
- Corporate and Development Group Expectations -Various types of demands from all sources -Corporate policies
- Organization specific design procedures and methods -Development constraints
- Technology constraints
- Operating and fiscal constraints
- Corporate, department, group, project and methodology standards

2. Environmental resources including:

- personnel

- materials -space -energy -facilities -training
- various types of information and data
- budgets -plans -schedules -work hygiene
- factors
- security factors

3. Outputs:

- Information -Questions -Models -Data
- Solutions -Plans -Training
- Procedures
- Methods -Methodologies -Discoveries -Metrics -Personnel -Reports
- Various types and forms of communications
- Data bases
- New enterprise organizations -Complete software designs

The Design Component's functions of input, transformation, output, and feedback and adjustment do not function as simple discrete activities completed once and then that's the end of it. Rather, they work together to form an iterative process which continues throughout the entire design process culminating in a software system's design. Hence, the character of the computer software design process is such that it goes far beyond the strictly defined and discrete phase like activity format that many hold it to be, a format consisting of clear lines which distinctly separate all the phases of design activity from each other.

In sum, we see that all the various types of input identified above work to form the Design Component and give it meaning through process. Through this "coming together", user, Development Group, and software design inputs infuse the Design Component during various iterative stages of the design process, or system problem solving activity. Moreover, through those inputs termed the Development Group, acting under the direction of an additional input termed the Charter, the Design Component transforms selected inputs into a software design, ready for program code, to produce a product or software solution for the client component of the larger corporate suprasystem, which is the final output of the development system, i.e., the Development Group and everything that contributes to its capacity for serving the client.

Input and Output According to Living Systems Theory

The preceding two lists highlighting the expected inputs and outputs of the Design Component are far from exhaustive and are limited to the immediate environment only. For example, these lists really do not take into account those inputs which may enter directly from the corporate suprasystem, i.e. the local community. Because each list can become so large as to be unmanageable, another way of expressing the relevancy of inputs and outputs appears in Living Systems Theory (Miller, 1978). Rather than listing the various inputs and outputs according to traditional approaches, LST speaks in terms of Information, Matter and Energy. Hence, Living Systems Theory provides a method of grouping the many types of inputs and outputs together to form three primary classes. All systems receive inputs and transmit outputs in one or more of these three forms, i.e., Information, Matter and Energy. Hence, Living Systems Theory provides a less cumbersome way of expressing potential large data domains Therefore, for this reason, designers should become familiar with each term.

Information

In respect of the discipline of software design, Information provides the possible spark which makes design the reason for being, and therefore, Information acts as the "Causa-in-fieri, i.e., meaning, the Component's cause or the cause of coming-to-be and in no small way the existence reality. Hence, Information feeds all those systems which contribute to the perpetuation of the Design Component's continued existence. Strictly speaking, Information does not provide meaning. For Information is diverse and when viewed collectively, becomes the repertoire of all possible categories of signals, messages, symbols, or patterns to be transmitted. Hence, Information informs an individual designer's freedom to choose in a particular situation among the current repertoire - as long as the repertoire does not consist of duplicate information in the Design Component, the receiver.

> Information pertinent to the activity of the Design Component determines the application, transformation, and output of matter and energy within the design Component as well as any other Information coming into, through and out of the Design Component itself.

Information can signify a meaningful collection of data as it undergoes transformation within the Design Component throughout the entire software design process. Examples of such Information include client requirements, mini-specifications, data flow diagrams, structured charts, pseudocode, legal constraints, technical constraints, budgets, operating procedures, technical knowledge, rules, expert knowledge bases, information resource libraries, training programs, charter specifications, project plans, standards, design and other project conventions, design languages, design data, analysis output, schedules, raw corporate data from other data files or information data bases, design tools and techniques, design methodologies, data products, and so forth. Today, in the corporate world of computerized information systems, Information means money. The greater the complexity of any design project, the greater the variability of Information entering the Design Component.

Matter

The Design Component's matter consists of everything which occupies space within the Component's boundaries. Miller (1978) offers a traditional view when he describes Matter as: "anything which has mass (m) and occupies physical space" (p. 11). In other words, Matter exhibits extension in space. Both Information and Matter enter into the Design Component as inputs and depart as outputs. But Information serves to change the Matter's application in the Design Component by the individual designers or to change the Matter itself. Hence, in philosophical terms, terms found in Section One, while Matter contains the potential for receiving new form, Information often actualizes this potential. Examples of such matter include: software designers, office equipment, computers or workstations, fixtures, partitions, printouts, physicalized designs, structured analysis outputs including data flow diagrams, context diagrams, written narratives, written policies, procedures, methods and other forms

of documentation, data models, and so forth. Matter originally enters the Design Component as input, and ultimately leaves as output.

Energy

Software design can be an arduous task. As such, design requires human effort, automated tools, a methodology, or group of methodologies, and many other resources. And to make all of these resources work, design requires energy. It requires energy to transform input into outputs and to facilitate this throughput operations. When talking about design, the term Energy refers to the actual effort required to perform the functions and activities of software design

(Miller, 1978). Hence, when we speak of design energy, we mean two aspects of the Principle of Energy Conservation. Hence, in software design:

1. Energy refers to the conversion of the Design Component's inputs into action to produce software designs;

2. Energy to the transformation of material inputs into

outputs.

As with everything else in the world, the amount of potential energy available to the Design Component to meet the demands of software design, is proportional to the matter available to the Design Component to do its job. Obviously, the Design Component requires energy to design software. If an insufficient energy level exists, correspondingly, an insufficient matter base also exists. One follows from the other.

The relationship between matter and energy is a complex one. In living systems, as everywhere else, mass and energy are equivalent (Miller, 1978, p. 11). Hence, in Living Systems Theory, matter and energy are expressed together as a unity unless one or the other is specifically meant (Miller, 1978). Examples of matter-energy required by the Design Component include: heat, light, water, minerals, vitamins, protein, foods, fuels, raw materials of various kinds, and so forth. Even systems with a mechanical component require matter-energy as when a computer requires electricity or an automobile requires gasoline. "Matter-energy and information always flow together" (Miller, 1978, P. 15). Information acts as the force which holds the Design Component together since information is negentropic (Miller, 1978).

9: The Environment as a Multisystem

Matter-energy and information represent everything that is moved from the Design Component to another component of the Development Group and between the Design Component and any component of the Development group's environment, which itself exists as a multisystem, for all environments exist as multisystems. When I state that the Design Component's environment exists as a multisystem, I am referring to a network of systems which have their own subsystems relationships to each other. Moreover, as with all systems existing in the same suprasystem, for a system's environment is that system's suprasystem, these subsystems relationships can form as peer relationships. This means that such relationships may exist as:

- Hierarchical
- Centralized, or
- Equalitarian

relationships within the same suprasystem. Hence, the Development Group's analysis component, or analysis subsystem, exists as a peer system to the Design Component, and so means the environment exists as a system consisting

of multiple subsystems.

The designation of "peer system" as used here does not carry the common meaning that most think of when they hold one person to be the peer of another - as when one thinks that another is an equal in some capacity or another. Using the Systems Models Approach (Banathy, 1973), peer relationships may exist as one of three distinct types of which only one infers the concept of equality. This is the equalitarian relationship in which all peer systems possess an equal authority or importance of role. Hence, no peer system possesses a superior role.

The hierarchical relationship speaks to the nature of one component in a suprasystem as being superior or subordinate to another. Hence, the Development Group's project management component participates in a hierarchical relationship with the Design Component because project management exist as superior to design. The centralized relationship is easy to figure out. For this relationship refers to the nature of one component, or subsystem, as being central to all the others. Hence, a centralized component exists as the principal central subsystem within any suprasystem.

Under the common expression of the term peer, the meaning of quality becomes the dominant theme. This theme is not carried over into the domain of the suprasystem where we speak of peer systems. For the Development Group's Design Component, the environment, i.e. The Development Group, certainly consists of all three distinctions of relationships.

Environmental Boundaries and Their States

Regardless of the mandates of the Design Component's charter, the component will not complete its mission if the components boundaries remain closed from its environment. Any system can be either open or closed. The Design Component exists as a closed system, and thus a sick system, if its boundaries are closed or shut off from its environment in such a way that any transaction between the Design Component and its environment, i.e. the development Group, becomes impossible. Whenever such an event occurs, the Design Component soon goes off of existence. After all, we have seen that the Design Component depends upon its suprasystem, i.e. its environment, for the matter, energy and information which permit the design Component to function.

If the Design Component will experience entropy if its boundaries experience perpetual closure. If we remember that a system's boundaries define or delimit the system's space and set the system aside from its environment, including the environment's full complement of entities, their relationships and attributes, we will see that the boundaries remain open to keep the system viable. But a caveat raises its head high here and warns us that a system's boundaries cannot be held too open; for then the system would lose its specific character as an individual component of its suprasystem. Hence, in this case, the system would once again face oblivion for it would become unstable, random, and unpredictable. For the environment and the component would be the same. Thus, we are told: "For practical purposes, we cannot speak of completely closed or completely open systems. Closedness and openness are matter of degree" (Banathy, 1973, p.8).

Boundary State Control

Since systems cannot become completely opened or closed, their boundaries require strict control. An appropriate level of boundary control exists in the Design Component in the form of:

- Project Plans,
- Quality Assurance and Control,
- Standards and Procedures,
- Methods and Methodologies,
- Schedules and ilestones,
- and so forth.

In short boundary control is provided by all the Design Component's facilities and devices which help the Component control the complexity, volume, and variability of the matter, energy and information, i.e. input, entering design from the environment and the transformed matter energy and information returning to the environment.

The rule in software design is simplicity. The Design Component maintains simplicity by attempting to close its boundaries. Since systems tend toward closure in relation to the degree of variability in matter, energy and information entering and exiting the system, meaning the more varied the input the more open the system and the less varied the input the more closed the system, the control of the variability and complexity of matter energy and information entering the system directly leads to "closure by control" (Newkirk, 1988, p. 87).

Closure by control simply refers to the Design Component's capacity to control, manage and adjust the breaks in the Component's boundaries by the adequate and correct screening and acceptance of the various forms of matter, energy and information introduced to the component by its environment. The nature of software design is such that the range of input complexity becomes limited only by the technologies and methodologies of the software design profession and the client's imagination as the client seeks a particular software product or problem solution. Regardless of the client's imagination, the Design Component still must function as a living system, a human activity system, which exists for a specific purpose as defined by the various project and corporate charters. Hence the Design Component must strive to maintain an appropriate level of adaptation.

The Design Component possesses the capacity to modify its operations, procedures and methodologies in response to relevant client and environmental contingencies. In this capacity, then, the

Design Component acts as an adaptive and self-regulating system which manifests the capacity to redefine its own project infrastructure according to the demands of business and technology

Adaptation is crucial to the success of the Design Component. If the Component fails to adapt, either the environment will accommodate it, or the Component will

cease altogether. In order for the Design Component to assure its success, and thus continued existence, the Component must consistently engage in feedback and adjustment, the central operational aspect of systems which represents the control loop mechanism of the any system, the mechanism simply termed systems control or control (Banathy, 1973).

Adjustments to the Component, its processes, structures or products, can be made on the basis of matter, energy or information obtained through the process of feedback. Systems control through feedback and adjustment provides the Design Component with a powerful method of ensuring the success of any design project. Therefore, the total design process becomes one of co-action between the Design Component and its environment. Hence, the systems aspect of feedback and adjustment empowers the Design Component with its capacity for behaving as an ordered human activity system

Systems Environmental Model Summary

The software Design Component of the Computer Software Development Human Activity System, referred to as the Development Group, represents a complex and dynamical system. To adequately understand the Design Component, consider the following concepts:

- Dominating

- Peer Relationships
- Suprasystem Relationship

System Processes

- Input and Output
- Feedback and Adjustment
- Trade and Accommodation

The Design Component Structural Model

Traditionally, systems were recognized by their structures. And structures were known by team memberships, boundaries, physical constraints, and locations without any reference being made to the environment at all. But when using the systems perspective, an observer must encounter a system's environment to really ascertain that system's full structure. As a true system, therefore, the Development Group's Design Component becomes known by its;

- Goals
- Functions
- Components.

These can only be known when an observer encounter's the Design Component's environment, the Development Group. The full charter of the Development Group imputes meaning to the Design Component.

Design Components' Goals

The Development Group exists to produce computer software or problem solutions requiring computer software. To meet this agenda, the goals of the Development Group, the Development Group performs specialized functions, i.e., analysis, design, program coding, software testing and integration, software implementation and sometimes even maintenance. But the performance of these functions requires the establishment of groups, or components, to attain the Development Groups goals. As we have just seen in our discussion about the environmental model, these functions are performed by specialized components termed peer systems of the suprasystem, the Development Group. "The Development Group "employs components that are capable of carrying out the functions required to achieve the Goals" (Banathy, 973).

The Design Component exists to meet the design needs of the Development Group. Accordingly, the Design Component has design as its goal and thus, in association and cooperation with the other components of the Development Group, contributes to the design of the required systems environment. Moreover, the Design Component's goal of assisting the Development Group in the attainment of the Group's goal makes the Design Component, as with all other Human Activity Systems, a goal seeking social system.

However, the Design Component is much more than this, for it also exists as a goal formulating system: "It is a system given birth by the necessity to meet a specific need presented by the environment" (Newkirk, 1987). The goals defined for the Design Component by the Development Group, i.e., the design of computer software, works to clarify the ultimate requirements of any Development Group client. Hence, helping clarify the needs of a client becomes a secondary goal of the Design Component. And clarifications often occur throughout the process of design as the Design Component exercises its own autonomy by formulating its own design goals according to the limitations imposed of all components by the project constraints.

In addition to the foregoing, i.e. the first two goals, the Design Component must attain a third goal as well. While the first two goals are essential to the absolute existence of the Design Component, and never vary, this third goal exists as a project specific goal. Hence, this goal varies with each project. By the third goal, I am referring to the goal of meeting the particularized project requirements, the schedules, quality levels, budgets, time, technology feasibilities, and so forth. For the Design Component certainly functions with the expectation of attaining each project's individual goals, goals which are centered more on the Design Component's project performance than on the existence of the Component as a Development Group subsystem. Regardless, of the goal being targeted, the Design Component can only remain successful as long as it functions appropriately to meet the demands placed upon it by each goal. This means that the Design Component must work hard to tailor its functions to support each specific goal.

Design Component's Functions

The identification of the Design Component's goals represents only one facet of understanding the Component's structure. We also need to examine how the goals are attained. In other words, the system's observer needs to examine the functions responsible for achieving the Design Component's stated goals.

When viewing the Design Component from a high level, the matter seems a simple one and the functional lines appear distinctly drawn. In the challenging reality that is software design, such a conclusion could not be further from the truth.

In practice, the dynamic and every changing infrastructure of each project actually determines the functional mix of the Development Group and by inference the Design Component. Sometimes the design function is redefined completely, or during software maintenance, the preliminary design function may be ignored altogether. However, regardless of the Design Components definition and redefinition, and regardless of each project's infrastructure, the Design Component as a system must perform the primary systems functions of:

- Input
- Transformation
- Output

Feedback and Adjustment

Without attending to these functions, the Design Component would quickly cease to exist as a Human Activity System - as we have previously seen when we examined systems boundaries. These four fundamental systems aspects provide the basic structure of any system; but they are not the only aspects which define the Component's structure. But they do contribute to its definition in a critical way. Other aspects termed specific-to-the-system functions combine with these four basic functions to help the Component form its full range of structures, generically and in support of each project. The ideal that every system has a structure should not be taken too lightly. For the structure of the system governs the system's evolution, and thus adaptation, over time.

Usually, we can model the structure by fixing our attention on the state of the system. The state is defined as the minimum information required to describe the system's condition in such a way that, if the input's re known, then the condition at any time is completely determined (Negoita and Ralescu, 1987).

For the Design Component, specific software design functions center around the activities of synthesizing information, building system's boundary models, designing structured charts, producing pseudocode, testing, conducting walkthroughs and other technical reviews in support of validation and verification, employing prototyping, and so forth. As specific to design as these operations may be, most, if not all, are still involved with the fundamental systems operations of inputting data, transforming it, outputting and controlling data. For example, when the designers receive analysis information to support the specific the design of structured charts, the designers are engaging in input operations, and then transformation when the mini-specifications become structured charts, followed by output to the client, and always feedback and adjustment.

Indeed, the four principal operations of systems remain pervasive throughout the entire design cycle. After all, the Design Component requires input to produce a detailed design. Moreover, the final detailed design exists as a transformation of such input, usually the mini-specifications into the design. Ultimately, the transformed detailed design becomes a formal output at the appropriate iteration of design. Feedback and adjustment control the entire design process from input to transformation to output. Nevertheless, this software development function, which exists as a set of the four principal aspects of systems in its own particular way, is termed detailed design.

If we fully understand what was just said, many implications become obvious. For all systems specific functions can be defined only by a detailed analysis of the Design Components goals. For example, a specific goal could be to design software which produces a running total of rerun time for all accounts payable applications. Such a goal certainly defines a systems specific function, a function which includes input, transformation, output, feedback and adjustment, and even information transmission operations.

However, these four principal systems functions exist in this case to support a specific Design Component function which itself was required to meet a specific client goal. In this case, transformation occurred because relevant systems-specific-functions were performed.

Hence, a practical software design must include both general and specific systems functions. If either be ignored, any problem solution or software product which results will be incompatible to the needs of any client. "Specifying functions is important. The more specifically we state functions, the better we are able to identify and select components that have the requisite capabilities (Banathy, 1973).

From what we already know about the three types of goals in design, we can see that the Design Component must concern itself with goals, functions and components - as well as needs, requirements and goals - from several levels simultaneously. The Design Component must not only concern itself with

all of these aspects of the Development Group in general, or with the client in particular, i.e., the Development Group must go wider in its concern for systems success.

For the Design Component, then, the four principal systems aspects act as the building blocks for all the specific-to-the-system functions. requirements and goals as well as the relationships inherent in forming an integral relationship of at least the functions addressed above. If we wish, we can link:

- Three distinct levels of goals
- Four principal functions, and at least
- Two components.

Hence, a description of the Design Component alone provides a solid platform upon which to conduct a systems description of the client system and the environmental Suprasystem, which often contains aspects of both the client system and the Development Group as a special HAS n its own right at any given point in time. After all, we can apply the concepts discussed above o all systems, regardless of a system's level in its Suprasystem. Or even regardless of its importance in a system's study, whether in the environment or directly in the subject system alone. Also, this is the case regardless of an observer's perception while describing the system in respect to the systems:

- Goals
- Functions
- Components

This applied to either, or both, the client and environment systems using the approach presented above. For all systems, designers consider the range of the following:

- Needs,
- Goals,
- Functions,
- Subsystems
- Connected Systems
- Designs
- Relationships
- Transformations
- Examinations
- Levels
- Components
- Operations

Functional Summary

Fundamentally, at the General Systems Level, the Structural Model's functions include:

- Input
- Transformation
- Output
- Feedback and Adjustment

- Information Transmission

As we have seen, Input includes anything entering the Design Component from its Environment, while Output includes anything being sent to the Environment from the Design Component.

- Transformation, which is a system's production function, includes the activation of all specific-to¬the-system functions which produce a real change in the input rather than a mere simple data restatement, which is often the case with mere information processing.
- Feedback and Adjustment includes the full system's control mechanism which keeps the Design Component on its critical-reliability path. Feedback and Adjustment operates as the basis system's control loop.
- Information transmission is associated closely with transformation and provides the Design Component with the capability of performing information exchange, as is the case when one peer system exchanges a resource with another peer system requiring that resource as a component of a larger system design.
- Specific-to-the-System functions are those which stand as unique to the technology of the designing system. For example, many of the specific software design goals expected by the client will require specific-to-the-system functions not commonly found in other systems, i.e., building a structured chart to develop a software design.

From a particular level of perspective regarding Structure, Human Activity Systems engage in several defining functions including:

- Input
- Transformation

- Output
- Feedback and Adjustment
- Information Transmission

The specific-to-the-system functions, i.e., designing structure charts, mirror the traditional approach of defining a software design component. However, using Living Systems Theory (Miller, 1978) we can bring the structural model to a lower level of detail. In this case, the primary systems operations of Input, Transformation, Output, and Feedback and Adjustment may be modeled to include the Matter, Energy and Information functions of Living Systems. Accordingly, the specific-to-the-system functions simply become iterations of these models.

10: Systems Functions in Living Systems Theory

Living Systems Theory, a remarkable work by James G. Miller (1978), views systems in respect to their structures and processes. Structure varies according to:

- Distinctions of shape
- Patterning of subsystems
- Components in space, size, color, constituent materials
- Other aspects of systems" (Miller, 1978, p. 51).

For Miller, then, a system's structure refers to: "the arrangement of its subsystems and components in three-dimensional space at any given moment in time" (1978, p. 22). And Process refers to:

> "all change over time of matter-energy or information in a system" (1978, p. 23).

Using the Systems Models Approach (Banathy, 1973), we model each as a Structural and Behavioral Model.

Processes

Earlier I wrote that the processes of the Design Component consisted of the four primary operations: input, transformation, output, and feedback and adjustment. Moreover, each aspect of the system's feedback Design Component engaged in specific-to-the-system functions which rested upon a foundation of the four systems primary operations. For example, the systems principal specific functions executed during the design of structure charts included:

- inputting preliminary design information,
- transforming such information into structured design documentation,
- sending the structured detailed design documentation, i.e. design models, back to the environment.

All of these operations occurred while the systems designers controlled the entire design cycle with loops of feedback and adjustment. Thus, Using Living Systems Theory, we are able to explode the four principal systems operations into subsystems which process either Matter, Energy or Information. Hence, Living Systems Theory, LST, focuses on six primary processes:

1. Process relationships between inputs and output;

2. Adjustment processes among subsystems or components, used in maintaining variables in steady states;

A. Matter-energy input processes;

B. Information input processes;

C. Matter-energy internal processes;

D. Information internal processes;

E. Matter-energy output processes; to

F. Information output processes;

G. Feedback.

3. Evolution;

A. Emergents.

4. Growth and Cohesiveness

5. Integration:

6. Pathology:

   A. Lack of matter-energy inputs;

   B. Excess of matter-energy inputs;

   C. Inputs of inappropriate forms D. lacks of information inputs;

   E. Excesses of information inputs of matter-energy;

   F. Decay and termination.

Each of these six processes revolve around input, transformation, output, and feedback and adjustment. Thus, the four primary functions of systems are enough to support any livings system's six fundamental processes. Furthermore, the application of LST's six processes to the observation and description of the Design Component's structure provides a more comprehensive foundation for modelling the components of the Design Subsystem itself.

The Design Component exists as a technical human activity system, a special type of social system. Thus, it maintains an individual life cycle marked by the pangs of evolution, growth, cohesiveness, integration and even decay and ultimate termination. In a practical sense, the Design Component becomes energized by its process relationships between inputs and outputs. Obviously, the Design Component strives to control the different categories of process relationships every time it works toward a goal by transforming inputs into outputs accordingly:

- Information inputs to produce information outputs
- as when mini-specification inputs are transformed into pseudocode outputs;
- Information inputs to produce matter-energy outputs as when data flow diagrams are transformed into physicalized data models;
- Matter-energy inputs to produce matter-energy outputs as when preliminary design models are transformed into detailed design models;
- Matter-Energy inputs to produce information outputs as when software design policies are transformed into software design standards.

Design proceeds as a dynamic process conducted by a Human Activity System, the Development Group's Design Component. To remain functional, the Design Component continually energizes appropriate adjustment processes. These processes help maintain a critical balance between itself and other Development Group subsystems or components and between itself and the external world. The balance is accomplished by the Component's systems control operations of feedback and adjustment which guide the Component to steady levels of design performance and acceptable software product designs. Hence, the Design Component energizes adjustment processes to control the "dynamics of design" (Banathy, 1984).

Central to the notion that design proceeds as a dynamic process, as mirrored in the six processes of Living Systems Theory above, Banathy (1984) offers "an image of the interaction dynamics of design inquiry".

In other words, Banathy demonstrates how the Design Subsystem's adjustment processes balance and control the "process relationships between inputs and outputs" including:

1. Matter-energy input processes;

2. Matter-energy output processes;

3. Information input processes;

4. Information output processes;

5. Matter-energy internal processes;

6. Information internal processes

7. All feedback processes.

Banathy pointed out that the dynamics of design occur as the designer traverses the "spaces of design" in an iterative and spiralic fashion. For, as Banathy explained (1984), the Design Subsystem itself exists as a complex Human Activity System consisting of several:

- Environments of design
- Spaces of design
- Systems of Design.

Together, these three aspects form the Design Subsystem's principal components. According to Banathy (1984), the aspects of design dynamics which traverse the Spaces of Design include the Dynamics of:

1. Iterative and Spiralic Design - design occurs through iterative cycles rather than by progressing through linear phases (Jones, 1963).
2. Feedback and Feedforward - design occurs as the designer

continually encounters the past to see how earlier accomplishments affect current happenings (Banathy, 1973).
3. Divergence-Convergence - design occurs as variability of alternatives is sought so that a final, workable alternative may be selected 1972).
4. Multi-Systemic Thrust in Design - design occurs under the systems perspective by encountering the environment and its various levels of systems (Banathy 1978).
5. Participative Design - design occurs through negotiations conducted by the many parties involved in design decision-making (Warfield, 1982).

Using Living Systems Theory (Miller, 1978) and the Systems Models Approach (Banathy, 1973), we are able to see that design signifies a total effort by a human activity system. The effort occurs as the design team continually visits the various spaces of design in an iterative and spiralic fashion. The processes outlined in Living Systems Theory, i.e., adjustment processes among subsystems or component used to ensure a steady state, support the Design Component's drive toward autopoiesis and project success:

Autopoiesis refers to the characteristic of living systems to continuously renew themselves and regulate this process in such a way that the integrity of their structure is maintained. Not only the evolution of a system, but also its existence in a specific structure becomes dissolved into processes. In the domain of the living, there is little that is solid and rigid. An autopoietic structure results from the interaction of many processes (Banathy, 1984, p. A-11 quoting from Maturana & Varela, 1975, p. 7)

Miller reasons that more effort has been directed to the study of process at all levels than to the study of structure (Miller, 1978). And yet, structure supports the processes. But what comes first, the definition of components from which processes occur? Or the design of processes which produce components to support them? Living Systems Theory identifies six basic processes. But what components support them?

Systems Components Through Living Systems Theory

Thus far our examination of the structure of the Development Group's Design Component, and hence our Structural Model, has studied the Design Component's goals and processes from the system's perspective. Earlier I even briefly identified the Development Group's components using the traditional model. Hence, he identified the traditional components of software development such as project management, analysis, design, coding, and so forth. However, if we have learned anything about systems thinking by now, we should realize that the traditional view provides a very weak paradigm at best for understanding the system-based activity of software design. For, no substitute exists for systems thinking when we must do design by engaging in systems thinking. Therefore, when considering the need for systems thinking while doing software systems design, the importance of describing the Design Subsystem's components from a systems perspective becomes indisputable. The passages that follow employs Living Systems Theory and the Systems Models Approach to describe the Design Subsystem's components, the subsystem components which are responsible for performing all the system's functions deemed necessary for achieving the Design Component's goals.

A system's components form that systems individual work groups. However, to remain a viable, functioning system, rather than a mere collection of individual work units, the components must absolutely attain a state of interdependency to such an extent that a whole system forms. Through such a fusion of components, a new entity emerges that equals more than the simple sum of all the whole system's components; or else there would not be a system. Banathy (1973) suggested two reasons for this:

1. The relationships of the components to each other;
2. The designed interactions that fuse the components into a system - for fusing elicits a change in the components to make them system-like (Banathy, 1973).

In the Design Subsystem, as in all other human activity systems, the systems functions, which are themselves determined by the system's goals, determines each the capabilities of each component. Hence, the need to perform structured systems design presents the Development Group with the need to have a component which can perform the function of Structured Systems Design. In this way, the function, which flows from the system's goals, defines the capabilities of the Design Component. Consequently, the relationships formed by the Development Group's components or subsystems to each other are themselves designed, and therefore not random. In this way, the components become connected by patterns of nonaccidental, purposeful interactions. These are, in fact, designed interactions.

The Design Component performs its many functions through the activation of its own components or the suprasystem, i.e. the:

- Environment,
- Operational goals of the software product or problem solution,
- Functions required to attain these goals.

Subsequently, the remaining Development Group subsystems receive the mandate to perform their own specialized functions, i.e. design, code, test, and so forth, to assist with attaining the client's goals. Hence, the client's goals define the functions which define the various software development system's components, and thus the entire Development Group (Newkirk,1987) of its own peer system network. In this mandatory "goal to function to component" development process, design remains intact. For the Design team, this means that Project Management calls upon the Development Group's analysis efforts to identify and define, beginning with the requirements from the organization, the design specifications.

Earlier, I defined the Design Component as an open system, meaning that the Component receives inputs from the environment through openings in the Component's boundaries. The boundaries set the design Component apart from its environment. However, being an open system, the Component also behaves as a dynamic system, as we have just seen. This means that the Design Component's properties continually experience flux and change.

Personnel come and go, new equipment appears and disappears, methods and procedures change, the knowledge base adapts to influences of technology, client's always want something new, the environment lays down new policies and budgets, ad infinitum. Even the fundamental element of design, the data itself, continually changes to provide clearer and more current information. The Design Component exists as a system in a turbulent environment to accommodate the dynamic realities of business and technology. Indeed, the Design Component itself grew out of the need for change in a changing world. Hence, the Development Group's subsystems continually exchange or transmit information and resources in parallel across systems-environment boundaries. Ultimately, such flux leads to a continuous change within themselves. This is the deepest character of Systems Design (Newkirk, 1987). Moreover, the Development Group's subsystems change, basically, marks the dynamic nature of the Development Group's Systems Design

Components. In Systems Design, little remains static. Change is the operational word and description of the design process.

The Design Component exists as a dynamic, open Human Activity System. This means that the HAS's own subsystems maintain a finely balanced state of interdependence. This state directly contributes to the Development Group's systems state termed component integration, a state which makes the Development Group a system marked by wholeness. Thus, a single change in any one group component ignites numerous changes in the other group components. In a human activity system, interdependence and integration exist as finely balanced attributes of a whole system. If the balance evaporated, the system would fall apart into many separate, closed systems. And each in turn would soon cease to exist. For this reason, a strong movement towards interaction and interdependence remains necessary, a movement leading to a synergistic integration through which the Design Component assimilates the entire Development Group's identity.

For the Design Component, a highly developed, well defined, systems infrastructure will contribute to the success of the Component's drive toward full integration and interdependence. This means that the Design Component does not simply exist as a design component, but now, since it exists as fully integrated into the Development Group, the Design Component exists as a software development Design Component. Thus, it exists as a design component performing the function of software design. If the balance of integration fails, the entire

Development Group fails. However, if integration and interdependence succeed, a state of systems wholeness now firmly exists.

> "Wholeness means that although we can think of systems as being evolved from parts, once the system has evolved, it is indivisible" (Banathy, 1973).

The Design Component maintains appropriate levels of integration, interdependence, and balance through the six living systems processes outlined previously. This means that integration, interdependence, and balance become additional Design Component goals. Moreover, the processes which seek to attain these goals can only be energized by specific components dedicated to the performance of the associated processes. Living Systems Theory identifies 19 systems essential to the functioning of the Design Component's

processes. These 19 systems are dedicated to processing matter, energy and information, the Design Components inputs, outputs and resources.

A Description of the Design Component's 19 Critical Subsystems:

The Design Component exists to respond to the Development Group's software design needs directly and the client's needs indirectly. Depending on the organization, these needs range from the simplest to the most complex. Hence, the Design Component's organizational structure must be such as to permit it to respond quickly, efficiently, and effectively to the client community's diverse demands and the corporate strategic imperative. As we have already seen, this means that The Design Component must consist of a number of critical subsystems which support the dual initiatives of performance and response: perform the activities mandated by the Development Group; and respond to any acceptable client request according to the

Development Group's directives. To meet these initiatives, the Design Component must contain a complexity level equal to that of the organization it supports.

Indeed, the 19 systems identified as Living Subsystem do not exist in the Design Component alone but must exist in every living system if it is to remain viable. As we will see in Section Three, Living Systems Process Analysis (Collen, 1987) examines the 19 critical subsystems of any living system and helps an observer determine the rate and range of the Design Component's effectiveness as the Component works toward the achievement of its goals, i.e., the satisfaction of the Development Group's and client's needs. In the process, Living Systems Process Analysis answers two important questions:

1. Who participates in the subsystem process?

2. What does each person do to make the process happen?

To answer these questions, Living Systems Process Analysis concentrates on the "traditionally defined organizational entities and general flows which are involved in carrying out the process" of each critical subsystem (Collen, 1987). These general flows are found in the six Living Systems processes identified earlier, the system processes which perform input, transformation, output, and feedback and adjustment on matter, energy and information. The 19 different subsystems of a living system fall into three general classes. We will take a quick look at these subsystems:

1. Subsystems which process both matter-energy and information.

2. Subsystems which process matter-energy.

3. Subsystems which process information.

11: Matter-Energy and Information Subsystems

Reproducer Subsystem

Earlier I stated that the Design Component existed as a result of a corporate mandate to do software design, the charter. The Reproducer Subsystem made this happen. This system bears the responsibility for given birth to the Design Component and for reproducing the Component in any other corporate segment if indeed it exists elsewhere. In classical thought, borrowing from our previous discourses on Philosophy, this subsystem acts as the "causa-in-fieri", the cause of coming into being or coming to be. Hence, the Reproducer Subsystem acts as the first cause of the design Component's existence as a system in the order of extensional reality, meaning, as a concrete living system in time and space.

Boundary Subsystem

As the Design Component's initiation proceeds, the need to control the Component's boundaries immediately arises. Since the Design Component exists as an open Human Activity System, its boundaries require careful regulation. The boundaries must be kept open, but not too open. The Design Component requires a system to support the Component's drive to maintain a state of dynamic equilibrium and thus remain negentropic. For the Design Component, the Boundary Subsystem controls the mechanism which keeps the Component's members together as a system distinct from other organizational systems. In doing so, the Boundary Subsystem inputs and outputs matter-energy and information between the Design Component and its suprasystem, i.e. between the Component and its peer systems within the Development Group.

The success of the Boundary Subsystem in meeting its specific goals for the Design Component to a large extent determines the ultimate success of the Design Component, and ultimately by extension, even the Development Group - because the Boundary Subsystem largely determines the security levels of the Design Component's boundaries. After all, the Boundary Subsystem exists to protect the Design Component's boundaries from all forms of violation and define for the Development Group's peer systems, the extent of the Design Component's boundaries. The Boundary Subsystem includes the five basic flows of materials, services, communications, money, and personnel. Hence, it exists as a matter-energy and information subsystem.

For the Design Component, aside from personnel and relevant forms of energy, communications become the most critical flow. In the Design Component, communications takes on the form of the project plans, the quality management plan, the Component's functional procedures, the design methodology, schedules and milestones, the formal charter and directives, and all the other communications facilities which empower the Component, in cooperation with the larger corporate structure, to control the complexity and variability of all inputs entering the Component from the full environment and the transformed output returning to that same environment.

The Boundary Subsystems provides the Design Component's boundary identifies as the:

- Command,
- Communications,
- Control and

- Cooperation

protocols. This "four C" mechanism provides for the need to maintain boundary simplicity through "closure by control". Closure by control signifies the highest level of functional integrity that can be achieved by the Design Component through the Boundary Subsystem in that it provides the Component with a mechanism for controlling the variability and complexity of the inputs. Closure by control simply refers to the capacity of the Design Component to control, manage, and adjust the breaks in its boundaries by the correct screening and acceptance of the numerous inputs entering from the environment.

Fundamental to the process of dynamic equilibrium, the Boundary Subsystem employs the quality management plan as a formal guideline and method to maintain closure by control. Hence, this plan acts as a control mechanism that supports the Design Component's need to formally adjust the breaks in the Component-Environment boundaries. In doing so, the Component with an appropriate mechanism for sustaining quality management plan directly assists in controlling the variability and appropriateness of the design inputs, throughputs, and outputs. Moreover, this plan serves as an important feedback and adjustment mechanism as it enhances the Design Component's capability to adjust, control and manage not only the most frequently changing inputs, as when the discipline itself.

In this sense, then, the Design Component remains an adaptive and self-regulating human activity system. Through the its Boundary Subsystem, the Component possesses the capacity to protect and redefine its project infrastructure, and thus its organizational boundaries, according to the demands made by each individual client requirement, the corporation, and business and technology at large.

Adaptation is crucial to the Design Component's success. If the Component were ever to become incapable of adaptation, the Development Group would be expected environment course of Component's demands of modifies the inputs in midstream during the immediate design activity and the product outputs in relation to the changing the environment, but also to adjust itself to the ever-changing technology of the design to carry the burden of accommodation. Or the Design Component would cease to exist. For the Component, the principal mode of adaptation exists as closure by control. Closure by control marks the Boundary Subsystems' fundamental activity. Furthermore, the Boundary Subsystem's control loop mechanism functions through its various feedback and adjustment operations.

These operations constitute the system's control process. Hence, systems control, mediated by the dual operations of feedback and adjustment, provides the Design Component's means of insuring that the final design output conforms to the client's requirements. In short, the Boundary Subsystem by controlling and protecting the Component's boundaries, acts as the harmonizing mechanism of the Design Component within its environment. Thus, the entire design process becomes a process of coaction between the Design Component and its environment mediated by the Boundary Subsystem.

12: Systems Which Process Only Matter-Energy

The Design Component depends on matter-energy for its continued existence as a viable Human Activity System and for the resources which permit the Component to achieve its goals. The structure of the Design Component includes eight subsystems which are dedicated to processing only matter-energy. These include:

Ingestor Subsystem

This subsystem consists of all those persons responsible for bringing people, material, vendors, software design technology, hardware, power, supplies, and all other physical inputs into the Design Component. The means that for the Design Component, the Ingestor Subsystem acts as a management and procurement system. In many cases, due to the highly sophisticated nature of contemporary software design environments, and to assure the technical environment's integrity, the Design Component's management must maintain control and direction of the Ingestor Subsystem's responsibilities. The Ingestor Subsystem includes all those who share responsibility for bringing the full complement of physical resources into the Design Component. Elements of this subsystem may include the following:

- Human Resources Groups
- External Vendors
- Peer Systems Within the Development Group
- Other Corporate Human Activity Systems.

Distributor System

After the Ingestor Subsystem brings matter-energy to the Design Component, the resources are then distributed to their appropriate areas. The Distributor Subsystem defines and oversees this process by managing the receiving and transfer functions governing the incoming matter-energy resources introduced by the Ingestor Subsystem. For software design, Distributor Subsystem members include: project management, technical services support, quality assurance and control, design services, and other corporate members.

Converter System

Whenever the Design Component receives matter-energy, i.e. physical resources, from the Ingestor Subsystem via the Distributor System, the Design Component must ensure that all such resources arrive in a usable form. The Converter Subsystem addresses this need. In Design, the Converter Subsystem consists of persons responsible for integrating the technology, i.e., hardware and software, to form an adequate design system. Moreover, this subsystem functions to bring the continually modified personnel baseline up to an adequate level of operational efficiency. Hence, the Design Component's training and maintenance staff represent the primary segments of the Converter Subsystem.

Producer System

For design, this subsystem consists in every member directly contributing to software design production and for maintaining the Design Component's dynamic equilibrium. Hence, through the association of the Design Component's members working as a Producer subsystem, inputs and outputs to and from the Component are ensure to provide matter¬energy to both maintain and effective state of design operations and to send outputs to the environment. The actual product transfers occur through a distinct process energized by the Extruder System. The Producer Subsystem merely prepares software designs for delivery.

Matter-Energy Storage System

This subsystem performs the function of storing matter-energy in the Design Component. This subsystem consists of all those responsible for storing and retrieving all such matter and energy.

Extruder System

This system works as a complement of the Producer Subsystem to send products to the environment. For design, this Subsystem consists of project management, designers, test personnel, quality assurance, client staff, vendor, and design conversion and programming personnel.

Motor System

This system provides the means through which the Design Component enacts with its environment and energizes itself. For design, this subsystem consists of:

- Project Management
- Designers
- Technical Support Staff
- Human Resources Organizations
- Senior Management, and
- Sometimes Even the Client Community.

Supporter System

This system consists of the physical elements associated with the design process. It consists of the physical plant components of walls, desks, floors, ceilings, partitions, and so forth. These physical elements control the Design Component's physical structure. Moreover, they provide concrete reality to the design function, an important characteristic for human activity systems. Hence, the Supporter System provides the Design Component a physicalization in the sense of space and rigidity.

III. Systems which Process Only Information

Fundamentally the Design Component exists as an important segment of the Information Age. This Component represents the Information Business in no small way. The Design Component depends on information to:

- Train design teams
- Train clients
- Meet Information Product Design Requirements
- Track and Measure Performance
- Manage Data Flows of Software Design
- Design the constraints that remain so critical to a design project

The dependence on the Design Component's proper functioning, and even its continued existence, are so significant that at least nine systems components are dedicated to the information processing function. These systems follow below:

Input Transducer

This subsystem brings information into the Design Component and works much the same way as the Ingestor System. The Input Transducer Subsystem consists of those individuals who bring client requirements into the Development Group and those who assist those individuals. Members of this subsystem include:

Client and Design Team Members

- Marketing Groups
- Project Management
- Librarian Control Personnel, and
- Other People Assisting the Design Process.

Internal Transducer

Frequently, the information provided to the Design Component through the Input Transducer system leads to additional internal information. The Internal Transducer Subsystem governs the information generated within the Design Component by managing the Component's network of internal information channels. For design, such information arises from feedback and adjustment operations and from the activities performed by the Development Group's other components, including the client and vendor communities.

For example, the analysis group receives information in the form of client requirements and transforms these into programming specifications via data flow diagrams, and so forth. Through the Internal Transducer Subsystem, the programming specifications are treated as internal information and thus sent to the Design Component.

Decoder System

As information enters the Design Component, it must be transformed into a form which conveys meaning and technical content. The Decoder Subsystem contains the:

- Staff,
- Tools,
- Technology, and
- Hardware

required to convert information containing technical and project content into a form meaningful to the Design Component. Hence, the language of the environment conveys information which must be translated into the language of the Design Component. The Decoder Systems performs the translation.

Channel and Net System

As information enters the Design Component, or transfers from one component to another, the information requires a delivery process to energize a relay network. The Channel and Net System provides such a process. For design, Channel and Net consists of:

- Computer Hardware and Terminals,
- Workstations,
- Information Media,
- Telephone and Other Communications System,
- Personal Communications through Formalized Meetings, and So Forth.

Associator System

This System exists as a conceptual system. The Design Component's Associator development activities, in the Component's field of knowledge, and in the specialized knowledge bases. The subsystem exists whenever the Component's training and Subsystem resides in the Component's Training

and Development activities form an association with any newly received information. Hence, the Component's members receive the new knowledge and associate it with any previously attained knowledge. In this way, the Associator Subsystem associates knowledge of the client's requirements with the technical knowledge of how to convert the requirements into a software design. Ultimately, the entire software development process becomes an association of one level and class of information with another. Moreover, this hybrid class of associated information becomes further associated with the tools, techniques, processes, design hardware and software, and the like to produce a final software design - which itself represents another type of associated information, information termed knowledge.

For design, then, the Associator Subsystem consists of the association of data, information, and knowledge with the tools, techniques, activities, organizations, structures, hardware and software, staff, and so forth, of the actual design process and its supporting Development Group hierarchy. This association forms an enduring network of software development processes intellectually experienced by the Human Activity Systems constituting the suprasystem, i.e., the environment, as a learned event of relationships.

Memory System

The Design Component's information storage elements form the Memory Subsystem. Through this system, the Design Component reserves all the information flowing throughout the entire Design Component for future use, for backup, or simply in compliance with management or corporate policy, or even governmental regulation. The Memory Systems consists of:

- Data bases,
- The library,
- Other files
- Documentation on all forms of media such as tapes and disks
- Human memory exists as a special element of this subsystem.

Decider System

This system serves the functions of regulation and control. Hence, its focus rests on the dual operations of feedback and adjustment. For design, this system consists of project management, quality assurance and control, client staff, executive management, auditors, and technical specialists. Moreover, this system includes the policies, standards, methods and procedures, technical criteria, vendor pronouncements, and client and managerial directives.

Encoder System

In terms of overall utility, the Encoder System makes software design meaningful to the client. This system changes the Design Component's internal technical information into a form understood by the client and other members of the Design Component's environment. The Design Component exists as a technical Human Activity System chartered to perform many specialized activities culminating in a software design. As such, it pursues its own technical language. But after the Component has finalized the software design, it then acts to get the design to the client in a client-centered language.

Current software design practice eliminates the Encoder Subsystem by delivering the design in pure technical form without changing it into a client-centered language. The author suggests that the Development Group itself requires a badly needed redesign.

Output Transducer System

This system performs the actual release of all outputs to the environment. Hopefully, it follows the Encoder Subsystem's activity. Customarily, the Design Component transmits finished designs to the Output Transducer Subsystem without energizing the Encoder Subsystem to change the outputs language. In this way, the Design Component weakens the Output Transducer System's effectiveness by energizing the Transducer Subsystem to send out information that has not been adequately encoded. But if the Design Component operates correctly, it employs various types of media to assist the Output Transducer process. This media includes:

- Computer data bases,
- Hard copy printouts,
- Electronic mail,
- Published directives, and
- Formally modelled systems descriptions.

In terms of human resources, the Output Transducer Subsystem commits to:

- Project Management,
- Technical Personnel,
- Quality Assurance, and
- Client Team Members

The systems just outline represent the basic subsystems energized by any viable Human Activity System. Hence, it reveals the "ideal" model for the Design Component. Those who work as software designers will see that several of the subsystems included in this structural model do not operate in today's software design environment. The current Design Component model exists and functions as a "parti-potential system", i.e. "a living system which does not itself carry out all critical subsystem processes" (Miller, 1978, p. 19) identified by Living Systems Theory as essential to systems viability. Regardless of the Design Component's structure, the 19 subsystems represent the basic components required to meet the design goals.

In the event that design may be performed by a partipotential system, that system must replace the missing functions by developing a symbiotic relationship with another system that will act as the "missing link". If the design system fails to do at least this much, it will soon cease to exist. But whatever the case, either totipotantial or partipotential, the Design Component must engage in design through the mediation of the 19 systems outlined above. Moreover, these systems must operate in clearly defined areas termed the "spaces of design" (Banathy, 1984). For design is carried out in designated areas termed the spaces of design.

Moreover, while the 19 systems work together to form the Design Component as it designs software, they themselves fall into specific technical categories termed the "systems of design" (Banathy, 1984). For the 19 systems of Living Systems Theory serve as the Generic Model of all viable living systems rather than of the Design Component alone. Hence, the systems of

design, which exist in their own specific environment, more appropriately represent those systems specific to the Design Component as it exists in itself and as the that Component exists in its environment, an environment which includes the spaces of design.

13: The Spaces of Design

Earlier, I wrote that design existed as a spiralic process seeking a dynamic equilibrium. Such an equilibrium was maintained as the Design Component explored the spaces of design through a process termed by Banathy (1984) as interactive dynamics. Banathy explained:

> The exploration of the contextual (often called problem) space and the knowledge space is ongoing. In addition to an intensive initial of the contextual and knowledge spaces, as solution alternatives emerge, we continue to draw upon information generated from the ongoing exploration of the contextual (problem) space. As design proceeds, we have an increasingly better understanding of what to look for in the contextual space, and information gained there begins to enlighten out design. The same is true with the knowledge base. We draw upon organized knowledge increasingly and more effectively as the questions we formulate become ever more clear and better informed by knowledge. Consequently, our exploration of the knowledge base becomes better focused. The experience space is the remaining arena that surrounds design inquiry and is also continually explored as we proceed with design. In the arena, we conceptually test the various design configurations and reality test the most promising one(s). The outcome of design is a representation or a model of the desired system. It represents an approximation or image of what may evolve if the system is actually developed. This model evolves as we test and display the most promising solutions (Banathy, 1984, pp. 4-7-4-8).

Here, Banathy clearly depicts design as a spiralic process of reiterative exploration. The spaces of design are visited and revisited through the interaction dynamics identified previously until a final solution exist, "a model of the desired system", an inductive model. Briefly, the spaces of design include:

- The Design Solution Space - This space exists as the result of defining the purposes and goals of the design. Hence, a systems purpose initiates the design process, after all design acts as a problem solving method of inquiry, and the system's goals terminate the process. The Reproducer Subsystem functions in this space.
- The Contextual Space - This space provides all the sources used during design. Banathy (1984) writes that all the sources used in the characterization of all the systems and problems relevant to design exist in the Contextual Space.
- The Experience Space - Exists as the design space in which alternative models are tested against reality. For, models are merely models and not actual reality. Earlier, the author summarized a few weaknesses associated with model building.
- The Space of Organized Knowledge - This space contains all the knowledge explored during the design process - both knowledge of design generally and knowledge of the particular design problem specifically. Knowledge, and its proper application, makes the design process successful. Hence, knowledge takes many forms and covers many diverse topics.

Systems of Design

The structural model presented so far describes the Design Component as a human activity system consisting of at least 19 subsystems. These systems exist in the Design Component according to the operations performed in the problem solution space. Hence, the problem solution space represents the remaining design spaces to arrive at a design solution. On a broader scale, which goes well beyond the actual Design Component's subsystem structure, design itself

progresses as the result of interactions between the systems of design, i.e., the environmental systems involved in any given design project, and the spaces

and environments of design.

In no small way, then, the systems of design, employ project specific spaces of design, constructed from the general environments of

the systems of design. Thus, a relationship between the Design Component, the systems and spaces of design, and the design environments cement the actual design structure to suggest a general structural model of design. According to Banathy (1973), the systems of design which interact with the actual design process include:

1. The system of ideas, aspirations, intentions or problems; or the existing problem embedded system;
2. The systems to be designed - the future system signifying the principal design focus;
3. The design system itself which produces the actual software design product;
4. The system of operations; the system energizes within the problem solution space;
5. The knowledge base system from which all the relevant knowledge flows into the design system to energize the system of operations within the problem solution space;

6. The design support systems which energize the actual design system through management and maintenance.

These six systems function within environments which provide the resources, i.e., matter, energy, and information, which collectively support the spaces of design. Accordingly, the environments include:

- The concrete environment of the problem system or idea system;
- The future system's conceptual environment which is to be modelled;
- The Design Component's concrete environment, or environmental model to be developed.
- The knowledge environment, an abstract environment containing the entire "knowledge stock" relevant to design as a disciplined inquiry (Banathy, 1984).

Design Component Structural Model Summary

The model just presented describes the computer software development human activity system's Design Component in terms of its:

- Goals,
- Functions, and
- Components.

Using the Systems Models Approach (Banathy, 1973), and Living Systems Theory (Miller, 1978), we have seen that the Design Component consists of at least 19 subsystems, and the Component interacts with other systems of design. Moreover, we have seen that these systems of design exist in a general environment from which the spaces of design are defined to accommodate each design project.

One last point needs to be stressed here before I continue with an examination of the Design Component's Behavioral Model. This point also addresses structure.

Design as Disciplined Inquiry properly falls into that domain termed "Decision-Oriented" Disciplined Inquiry. Hence, design gives rise to the production of synthetic entities. These in turn produce various types of systems, from the most abstract to the purely physical and even the machine systems. Whereas, Disciplined Inquiry carried out by traditional science remains "Conclusion-Oriented" in its search for knowledge, but Design Inquiry seeks understanding.

The Design Component's Behavioral Model

By now, our Design Component Model should be nearing completion. We have examined the systems environment of the Component's, along with the environmental components, including the Component's inputs and outputs. We have just completed an examination of the Component's system structure including the most vital relationships existing between the Component's many subsystems - along with the rationale which ties these together. Throughout the description process, I emphasized the necessity for building usable Design Component models. Models, as used here, means "a representation of some object or activity in a form which is similar in many, but not all, respects' (Mayon-White & Morris, 1982).

Hence, in keeping with the Systems Models Approach (Banathy, 1973), I have completed, at least in shell form, both a Systems Environment and Structural Model of the Development Group's Design Component. Now we must do the same with the Design Component's behavior. This means that we still need to identify and model the Component's state variables, the relationships between them: "To truly understand systems, we absolutely must examine their behavior and observe the change that takes place in their entities, their attributes, and their relationships over a period of time" (Banathy, 1973). I intended this segment of the book to provide the required Behavioral Model. Therefore, what we are really interested in here can only be expressed through a System's Operations Model. Previously, we recognized that the Design Component's fundamental operations consist of the general systems operations termed:

- Input,
- Transformation,
- Output, and
- Feedback and Adjustment.

Previously, we defined these terms when we examined the Structural Model's processes and placed them in the context of the Development Group's Design Component, a Human Activity System. We viewed these processes not so much as dynamic operations but more in terms of structural objects. Now we will examine the same operations, but from a dynamic view which brings the system's modeler, i.e. designer, a broader understanding of their nature as relevant to a full systems description.

Input Processing

Generally, input processing permits the Design Component to interact with its environment. This necessary interaction empowers the Component to control the scope of the inputs it receives. This in turn provides the foundation for determining which inputs contain a design relevant value. From this beginning, then, the Design Component receives all relevant inputs for eventual transformation through system activation and thus for eventual output.

The Design Component focuses on two primary input types: environmental inputs and Design Component inputs. Collectively, these inputs provide everything that the Component requires in terms of matter, energy and information - to perform its functions, attain its goals and fulfill its higher level purpose, in cooperation with its environment, the Development Group. For design, this means that input process operations permit the Design Component to obtain, clarify and accept, for transformation, only those inputs which appropriately support the client's goals and needs, and the Development Group's mission.

Additionally, input processing operations perform a vital function by energizing feedback and adjustment. After all, feedback often becomes another formal environmental input. Without such input being received as feedback, system's adjustment, of whatever sort, becomes unlikely. Hence, the risk of failure increases. Input processing tells us that the design Component, as an open system, communicates with the client, and the Development Group, both environmental peer systems. As the Component receives the input, primarily through the process of communications, the Component must:

- Analyze,
- Edit,
- Order,
- Store,
- Record and
- Verify
- Initiate Relevant Components

This process unfolds prior to disseminating the input to the subsystems. The identification operation occurs as all systems of design identify and define the system's inputs. Naturally, this involves the continuous interaction of the design team with the client community. Moreover, the Design Team engages in design as certain systems components initiate and facilitate the design process by engaging in the interaction dynamics of design, quality verification., and ultimately, activation.

Targeted input attributes such as exactness and testability can be measured through time. A summary of these state variables at any given point in time will reveal the state of the client's inputs, and implicitly the state of the actual design project, and perhaps even the client's state of understanding about its own needs and goals:

> When this set of "dynamics" is known, we can simulate any possible evolution in time by computing transitions from one state to another. The dynamics, in other words, is simply a state equation specifying that the state of the system at any moment is a function of the state and the inputs in the previous moment. Therefore, it seems that one of the analyst's jobs could be to find the state equation, or model. The next step is to transform the model into one or more statements as part of a program operating on data. These data are numbers.

Sometimes we have to cope with noncommercial data. Linguistic values like "many" or "high" are frequently used in scientific descriptions. Facing this new complication, the analyst has to translate words into numbers. This translation is known as the semantic approach. The analyst may also want to recommend those inputs that are supposed to determine a specified evolution in time (Negoita and Ralescu, 1987). A systems description of input processing would be incomplete if it failed to describe the input operation's three primary aspects interaction, identification and activation. Collectively, these three operations help determine the design relevant data.

After the Design Component receives the different inputs from the environment, it initiates the input processing operation in three distinct stages. The first, termed interaction, permits the Component to receive, qualify, record, and even store matter, energy and information, As the input passes verification and clarification, it becomes value added to design. If required, the Design Component will act to provide feedback to the client and solicit additional clarification. Followings input clarification, the Design Component proceeds to the second input processing aspect termed identification.

Identification operations act to qualify and quantify all systems inputs. During design input operations, as with all system input operations, the Design Component must clarify the client's fuzzy or soft systems requirements. Identification operations assist in meeting this objective. The systems-relevant inputs become true inputs after they have been assessed and identified as necessary to design. The assessment's outcome results in the identification of the system-relevant input with specified values to the system. The feedback process ascertains the correctness and adequacy of these identifications (Banathy, 1973).

Following identification, input processing next engages the activation operations. Activation does two things: first, it brings the identified input into the Design Component; secondly, activation energizes the design process by disseminating the right input at the right time and place. For design, activation loop integrity, i.e. input dissemination and design activation, remains acceptable through the intervention of feedback and adjustment. Here, feedback and adjustment act to ensure that the inputs from the environment do conform to the design requirements consistent with the current design iteration.

Input Processing Summary

The Design Component's input operations consist of three distinct operations: interaction, identification and activation. Each operation performs vital activities as it assists the Design Component during the input reception cycle.

Through interaction, the Component receives and verifies the environmental inputs. Through identification, the Design Component evaluates the inputs from the design system's point-of-view, selects the relevant inputs while qualifying and quantifying the input's values. Through activation, the Design Component disseminates the input and activates the design process with it. The input operation introduces the following entities into the Design Component:

- Those entities which will become the direct subject of transformation; "The subject is the part of the input that has to be transformed by the system from an input state to a specified output state" (Banathy, 1973).
- The Design Component's goals which mirror the final software product;
- Pertinent information about the client, the suprasystem, and even the whole corporation;
- Resources and facilities required to meet the client's needs, i.e., the software product or problem solution;
- The Design Component's operating constraints from the environment, design technology, corporation, community, i.e., experience space, knowledge space, the contextual space, and so forth. These constraints may consist of anything from management policies to technological limitations.

Living Systems Theory and Design Input Operations

As we have previously seen, according to Living Systems Theory (Miller, 1978) all systems consist of at least 19 subsystems. These systems process inputs in the form of matter, energy and information. Moreover, being systems themselves, all include the four primary systems aspects of input, transformation, output, and feedback and adjustment. However, where some systems process both matter-energy and information, others process only information or just matter-energy alone. By now, the meaning of matter, energy and information should be quite clear from an earlier presentation: matter refers to those things which occupy space; energy refers to the effort required to do work; information refers to the cause of a systems existence.

If we view the various systems aspects as ends in themselves, as if they existed in various systems as some sort of mini-requirements, we could look upon each of the 19 living systems as stressing the facilitation of one or another of these four aspects. For example, we have just discussed the systems aspect termed input and have broken it down into its component operations of interaction, identification and activation. The author submits, then, that while all living systems engage in input operations, some systems exist specifically for the sake of input processing, some for the sake of transformation processing, some for the sake of output processing, and some specifically to provide feedback and adjustment.

Input Specific Systems of Living Systems Theory

Systems which process matter-energy and information exist primarily to process inputs. Hence the Reproducer and Boundary Systems focus on input processing to impute existence to the Design Component. For without the concentration on input from these two systems, the Design Component would not yet exist, nor contain clearly defined boundaries. In a sense, then, neither the Component's existence nor boundaries could be a fact if the matter-energy and information systems failed to focus on the Component's earliest input stream. This input stream includes: materials, money, services, communications, and personnel. In addition to matter-energy and information systems, other systems focus on input processing as well. The following systems summary clarifies:

Input Specific Systems

I. Matter-Energy and Information Systems:

2. Reproducer System - processes start-up input;

3. Boundary System - processes systems configuration inputs;

II. Matter-Energy Systems:

- Ingestor System - this system exists specifically bring people, material, hardware, power, and all other physical inputs into the Design Component;
- Distributor System - operates to distribute the physical resource inputs to the Design Component's members;
- Matter-Energy Storage - operates to store matter- energy inputs in the Design Component;

III. Information Systems:

- Input Transducer - operates like the Ingestor System but only on information;
- Internal Transducer - operates on input originated within the Design Component itself;
- Channel and Net - operates on input to deliver it to where it should be used;
- Associator - operates to link all newly received information with existing knowledge bases; hence, the knowledge environment inputs information to build upon the Component's knowledge space;
- Memory Storage - operates to receive information and store it for future use;

We can see that of the 19 systems presented by Living Systems Theory, ten are primarily dedicated to the system's input aspect. For consistency sake, storage and throughput operations exist as aspects of input processing. The remaining nine systems support the transformation, output, and feedback and adjustment system's aspects.

14: Transformation Processing Operations

In no small way, transformation operations form the central design focus. Through this operation, the Design Component produces the software designs required by the development Group and thus attains its immediate project goal. By energizing transformation, the Design Component transforms the various inputs received from the ten systems above into a computer software design according to the accepted client specifications passed to the Design Component from the analysis system. Transformation, the production operations of design, consists of three complementary operations: "Transformation has three major interacting and interdependent domains" (Banathy, 1973, p.44): transformation production, transformation facilitation, and transformation control and adjustment

Transformation Production

Through Transformation Production, work on the design inputs to transform them into the required software designs. In no small sense, then, transformation production "is where the action is". During this design segment, the Design Component employs design technology, according to the development Group's general development methodology guidelines, to perform "specific transformation production operations". This class of operations, energizes the design components to perform the requisite activities in an interactive mode which harmonizes the total Design Component efforts.

Left to themselves, however, the Component's "specific transformation production operations" remain insufficient to bind the Component's members into a unified form. The systemization-integration operations do this. However, these operations do not directly contribute to the production of a software design but instead serve to bring the Design Component to an essential state of operational integrity or wholeness. Through progressive integration and systemization, systems components take upon themselves increasingly more the characteristics of the total system, and in so doing they lose their original input characteristics and initial independence as they become ever more involved in the system (Banathy, 1973).

Transformation Facilitation

During actual design, design management must work to maintain a dynamic equilibrium between the various design subsystems. Integration must be continually balanced throughout the entire design process. Transformation facilitation operations assist in the performance of this task. These operations allow managers to energize only those aspects of design as the are required and only to the extent that they serve the design process in conformance to the client and project constraints.

Transformation Control and Adjustment

Transformation and Control operations provide the mechanism for maintaining the dynamic equilibrium energized by transformation facilitation. While the system's feedback and adjustment aspects speaks mainly to the control interactions between the Design Component and the Development Group, its environment, transformation and control operations address the Design Component's own internal control in respect to its design subsystems. Hence, design introduces a comprehensive monitoring process which provides the foundation for any other control and adjustment operation. As Banathy points out:

> Monitoring, measuring performance, analyzing the data, and adjusting in order to correct for deficiencies constitute the performance-effectiveness dimensions of transformation control" (1973, p. 47).

The mechanism which performs the monitoring, analysis and adjustment functions exists as transformation control. Transformation adjustment makes such control practical. Adjustment operations focus on the transformation operations with an eye toward their continual improvement. Without the systems integrity provided by the transformation control and adjustment operations, the Design Component degenerates and Trist put it this way:

> In contradistinction to physical objects, any living entity survives by importing into itself certain types of material from its environment, transforming these in accordance with its own system characteristics, and by exporting other types back into its environment. By this process the organism obtains the additional energy that renders it "negentropic"; it becomes capable of attaining stability in a time¬independent steady state - a necessary condition of adaptability to environment variance (Emery, 1965).

Transformation adjustment and control provide design the capability of altering the Design Component's internal operational structure. The Design Component performs these operations in cooperation with the Development Group at large. If the Component acts independently, it soon undermines not only itself but this event, the Design Component would quickly become incapable of meeting client community's software needs. After all, as Myon-White and Morris remind us:

> "The components are affected by being in the system and the behavior of the system is changed if they leave it" (1982).

Transformation Specific Systems of Living Systems Theory

We have already seen that Living Systems Theory presents ten systems focused on the system's aspect termed input operations. This leaves nine systems dedicated to the last three primary systems aspects. In Living Systems Theory, transformation centers around the essential change of inputs into a form of outputs that are now suitable to preparation and transfer to other system's components as inputs. Now I will outline the three living systems focused on transformation.

Transformation Specific Systems

I. Matter-Energy Systems

- Converter System - operates to transform matter¬energy inputs into a form that is acceptable and usable to the Design Component;

II. Information Systems:

- Decoder System - operates to transform information inputs into a form that conveys meaning or technical content and that can be used for design;
- Encoder System - operates to change internal design information into the language of external information users, i.e., the client, the Development Group, and so forth;

Output Operations

Output operations signify the design's terminus or end-point:

> Output operations concern the identification and assessment of systems-relevant output and the dispatching of this output to the environment or to systems control and adjustment" (Banathy, 1973, p. 40).

Output operations signify the final operations in a long line that began with the client's request. As with many operations previously described, output design employs a cyclic process which produces various levels of products before sending a final design to the client, from preliminary to detailed levels. Hence, output operations generally produce several versions before the final design meets client acceptance. These operations include: identification and assessment operations and dispatching operations.

Identification and Assessment Operations

These dual operations provide the mechanism for ensuring that the client receives exactly what the client requested. This means that the final deliverable must be both relevant and adequate. However, the operations function in an iterative manner. However, the output assessment presents a difficult challenge. Criteria must be defined, output models must be updated, or even complete rebuilding, measurements must be taken, and reviews must be employed. Throughout, identification and assessment, the focus remains on relevancy and adequacy.

Dispatching Operations

Upon the completion of identification and assessment, and if all goes well, design energizes the remaining output operation. This operation exists as the dispatching operation. When the Design Component determines that the output is both relevant and adequate to the client's demands, the Component sends the output to the environment, whatever that environment may be, from the Development Group itself to the client community.

Output Specific Systems of Living Systems Theory:

The Design Component depends on matter-energy and information for its continued existence and for the resources which permit it to achieve its goals environment and client satisfaction through innovative software design. However, nothing gets accomplished until the design products finally work for the client. Living Systems Theory identifies several systems that function to get output where they belong. These include:

I. Matter-Energy Systems:

- Distributor System - operates to distribute matter-energy to the appropriate receiver system; depending on an observer's frame of reference, this system can be classified as either an input or output system;
- Extruder System - operates with the Producer System to get products out of the Design Component;

II. Information Systems:

1. Output Transducer System - operates with the Encoder System to send information to the environment.

- Feedback and Adjustment Operations

These operations provide design with its particularly identity as a system. Moreover, these operations keep open systems open. The most significant difference between enterprises that operate as systems and those that do not is that systems are controlled by design through feedback and adjustment operations" (Banathy, 1983, p. 51). In short, a system exists as a relation between input and output mediated by a controller. Feedback and adjustment is such a controller and consists of five distinct operations:

1. Monitoring the system and its output for adequacy;

2. Analyzing and interpreting the results of all monitoring activities;
3. Determining any adjustments and constructing appropriate models;
4. Identifying and defining the adjustment consequences;
5. Implementing the appropriate adjustments.

As a group, these five feedback and adjustment operations touch upon every systems aspect from input to output. In this sense, then, feedback and adjustment exist as the Design Component's global operations.

- Monitoring Operations:

These operations provide feedback and adjustment the data required to improve the behavior of the Design Component by continually measuring the state of the the design process at any given point in time. These operations employ specific metrics which reveal the design attributes contained in the developing design. For the Design Component, these metrics reside in three sources:

1. The output metrics obtained from identification and assessment operations;
2. The design system's operations metrics, as it visits and revisits the design spaces, obtained transformation and control operations;
3. The environmental impact assessments obtained from environmental evaluations, i.e., design performance evaluations and design output evaluations. From these, the Design Component can then extrapolate its posture. t is perfectly clear that the state of the system determines its output, which in turn determines the state of the feedback and, therefore, the system's input adjustment" (Negoita and Ralescu, 1987).

- Analysis and Interpretation:

To find meaning in the evidence obtained through monitoring, the Design Component needs to analyze and interpret any findings. The Design Component analyzes the evidence from the perspective of possible discrepancies between the design products and the client's requirements. Discrepancies can be quite varied ranging from data inconsistencies to unknown technology constraints. The Component's interpretation of these findings should go all the way to the discrepancy's source.

- Determining Adjustments and Constructing Models:

Adjustments can take the form of either negative or positive feedback. Normally design employs negative feedback to keep the products within predetermined constraints. However, the types of feedback employed have a direct bearing on the adjustment model developed by the Design Component in response to the evidence collected, analyzed and interpreted.

The Design Component constructs an adjustment model to improve the design by closing the gap between the expected design and delivered design. Such a design can be either a narrative, a diagram, or sometimes even a complex display. Whatever the case, the model must be focused on the corrective measured identified during interpretation. Subsequently, the models must pass the dual tests for relevancy and adequacy.

- Identifying and Defining the Adjustment Sequence:

These operations are important because they identify the consequences associated with design adjustment. Accordingly, alternatives must be looked at and risks assessments must be conducted. Nothing should be left to chance. The Component even requires a change control mechanism to control the adjustment process. Many complex issues will have to be raised; and all will have to be resolved.

Implementing Appropriate Adjustments:

Following the selection of the adjustment model, The Design Component must support its introduction very carefully. Obviously, changes should not be initiated randomly. This would only increase the complexity of the already existing design and perhaps lead to its failure altogether. Administrative and logistical concerns appear to be the most common issues facing the effort to implement adjustments to on-going designs. The technical side normally has the easier assignment.

- Feedback and Adjustment Specific Systems of Living Systems Theory:

Living Systems Theory presents several systems focused on feedback and adjustment operations. According to the Theory, living systems strive to maintain a state of dynamic equilibrium. Feedback and adjustment serve this need. Accordingly, such systems include:

I. Matter-Energy Systems:

Motor System - operates by assisting the Design

A component moves itself - as for example whenever the Component adjusts its behavior in response to feedback.

II. Information Systems:

Decider System – function to maintain regulation and control; feedback and adjustment represent the Design Component's control system.

15: Design Summaries

Summary of Feedback and Adjustment

Feedback and adjustment operations give the Design the guidance e required to deliver the required system design. While transformation control and adjustment speak to control and adjustment within the Component only, feedback and adjustment focus on all the communications, control and adjustments between the Component and its environment. For the Design Component, feedback and adjustment represent the central operation of the entire design process. As such, it performs several fundamental operations including: analysis and interpretation, data collection, adjustment modeling, risk analysis and threat assessment, change and version control, and so forth. Without feedback and adjustment, a system becomes only a procedure. A component its distinctive character as an open system.

Evolutionary Guidance Systems

Earlier, when examining the Systems of Design, I mentioned something about the system of goals and aspirations. Following Banathy (1984), we saw that this system comprised the design context. When we contemplate the design context, we have to wonder what energizes this context to achieve the goals and aspirations of any design system? In other words, where do we find the roots of the deeper human longings which drive any person to achieve the goals and aspirations of any design context? Briefly, such deeper human longings flow from the dimensions of one's personal Evolutionary Guidance System, or EGS. I will examine the Evolutionary Guidance System more closely in Section Three, for now we should understand that an EGS represents probably the most significant system of design. An

Evolutionary Guidance Systems transforms any design system from a control driven Human Activity System into a motivationally oriented Human Activity System (Banathy, 1987a).

Systems of Design and Their Living Systems Profile

We have previously seen that according to Living Systems Theory, all Human Activity Systems must consist of at least 19 critical systems to remain viable. The same applies to the Systems of Design since they too exist as Human Activity Systems, either as real-world systems or abstract systems. Although all viable living systems consist of the 19 systems types, each Human Activity System manifests a unique profile generated by a certain set of the 19 systems that exists above and beyond all the rest. For example, according to Living Systems Theory, the System-To-Be-Designed, an abstract system, must consists of at last 19 critical systems to be viable. However, above and beyond this consideration, the Systems To-Be-Designed manifests a profile that presents such a system as an "Outcome Event", meaning that this system represents the product of other systems. Hence, in a particular way, the essential nature of the System-To-Be-Designed comes-to-be through the primary interactions of the living systems types termed Matter, Energy and Information Systems. For these systems exist as Reproducer and Boundary Systems which share responsibility for the generation of new systems.

In a like manner, the remaining Systems of Design manifest a particular essential profile. This profile, derived from the preeminent interactions of a particular set of the 19 living systems, marks any System of Design as a specific System Event, as when The Design System exists as a "Transformation Event", meaning that this system primarily exists to design through transformation the "Systems-To-Be-Designed". Hence, from a particular point-of-view, the Design System comes-to-be through the primary interactions of the living systems types termed Information Systems. The remaining Systems of Design follow a similar pattern in obtaining their essential profile.

Summary of the Behavioral Model

I have just completed a Behavioral Model outline for the Development Group's Design Component. In reality, many discrepancies arise. For one thing, the Design Component often fails to energize an Encoder System. Rather the Component expects the environment to adjust to the Component's own technical language. In other cases, the design methodology most often fails to match the system type employing it or even the system type undergoing design. No wonder software development has such a poor record of achievement.

We have just seen that the Design Component exists as an open Human Activity System. A Design Component containing closed boundaries signifies a pathological Human Activity System, a system well on its way to becoming nonfunctional. Moreover, as a system, it consists of the four system's aspects recognized as input, transformation, output, and feedback and adjustment. These four aspects signify the Behavioral Model's principal verbs. At a lower level, we have even seen that these four system's aspects alone contain component operations - as when the input operation consists of:

- Interaction,
- Identification and
- Activation.

Collectively, these operations form the subsystems that are necessary in a system defined in the root definition, and to structure the verbs in a sequence according to logic" (Checkland, 1981, p. 170).

Summary of Creativity as Design

I submit that what we have just seen forms the Environment, Structure and Process of design. If we would do the same thing for "creativity", meaning, that which most authorities mean by creativity, we would form a "minimum list of verbs covering the activities which would find that the model would be remarkably alike. So much so as to be indistinguishable from each other. Creativity is design. Design is creativity. But in the pure sense of the term, creativity is a myth. Speaking about the close fit between design an art; a traditional creative expression, Banathy (1984) refers to Sless:

> Sless (an arts scholar) considered the subtle and simple difference between the arts and design. He defined design as the "process of originating systems and predicting their fulfillment of given objectives"; and art as "unspecified experimental modelling" (Sless, 1978, p. 123)

In many instances, I have found that at the most fundamental level of practice, design is an example of "unspecified experimental modelling". Obviously

It is certainly a "creative-like" human activity. Simon (1969) reminds us that "professionals are creating artifacts that respond to the requirements of the task environment and to the properties of the materials or resources used (Banathy, 1984, p. 1-11). Banathy himself reasoned:

> Design seeks to bring about a better future. It shapes and reshapes images of the world that can be or ought to be. Design explores and devises systems that

> design can be grouped with other art forms to attain goals, and it seeks out paths leading toward them. Design is a process of creative and disciplined decision-oriented inquiry (Banathy, 1984, p. 4-1).

> I think that design and creativity are from the same family. Indeed, they are identical twins. They are so close in fact that creativity is design. Remember this, many have much to say about design, including what it is; and many have much to say about creativity, but few render a guess to say what it is. In my mind, creativity implies myth; design expresses reality. (Newkirk, 2026).

One Last Look

Design signifies a path to reality which offers considerable understanding, and even some knowledge. Design as a human activity system represents complex behavior, unconscious as well as conscious, heuristic as well as spontaneous, direct and indirect, complex and simple. When taken to an appropriate level of detail, design itself becomes a formidable model of human capability, a cosmological expression of the human capacity to be "creative-like".

The Final Model

I. Domain of Disciplined Inquiry: Decision-oriented.

II. Transphenomenal Realm of Design: Synthetic Entities.

III. Environments of Design:

- Ideas or problems environment, the Design Genesis Environment;
- Future system environment;
- Knowledge environment;
- Design System environment.

IV. Spaces of Design:

- The contextual space;
- The experience space;
- The organized knowledge space;
- The problem solution space; 5. The inspiration space.

V. Marks of Design:

- Purpose, goals, organizing perspectives - the beginning;
- The design model - the terminus;

VI. The Interaction Dynamics of Design:

- Iterative and Spiralic Design;
- Feedback and Feedforward
- Divergence-Covergence;
- Multi-Systemic Thrust in Design; 5. Participative Design;

VII. Systems of Design:

- Design Inquiry or systems of operations;
- The future system, the system to be designed;
- The knowledge base system;
- Design support systems;
- The design human activity system;
- The existing system to be redesigned, the Design Genesis System;
- The Systems of Design Testing;
- Evolutionary Guidance Systems;

VIII. Systems of Design and Their Profiles:

- Design Inquiry: Transformation Event through Information Systems;
- The Future System: Output Event through Matter, Energy

and Information Systems.

- The Knowledge Base System: Input Event through Information Systems.
- Design Support Systems: Feedback and Adjustment Event through Matter, Energy and Information Systems.
- The Design System: Transformation Event through Information Systems.
- The Design Genesis Systems: Input Event through Matter, Energy and Information;
- Design Testing System: Feedback and Adjustment Event through Matter, Energy and Information;
- Evolutionary Guidance System: Feedback and Adjustment Event through Matter, Energy and Information.

IX. The Models of Design:

1. Environmental;

A. System entities and their functions;

a. environment;

b. boundaries;

c. input;

d. output;

B. Relationships;

a. suprasystem;

b. multisystem;

c. peer systems;

d. hierarchical;

e. centralized;

f. equalitarian;

g. subsystems;

h. components;

i. open;

j. closed;

k. closure by control;

l. self-regulating;

m. adaptive;

n. adjusting systems;

C. System Control;

a. adjustment;

b. accommodation;

c. termination;

d. feedback;

e. expected and actual states;

f. ordered state;

g. drives;

h. system control;

i. system environment coaction;

2. Structural;

A. Goals;

a. need;

b. requirement;

c. resources;

d. constraint;

e. environmental serving;

f. self-serving;

g. function identification;

B. Functions;

a. needs, requirements, goals;

b. general systems functions;

c. specific-to-the-systems-functions;

d. systemization;

e. transformation;

f. production;

g. information transmission;

C. Components

a. relationships;

b. designed inteactions;

c. independence;

d. progressive segregation;

e. progressive integration;

f. progressive interdependence;

g. systemization;

h. interdependence;

i. wholeness;

j. living systems

3. Behavioral;

A. Input;

a. interaction;

b. identification;

c. activation;

d. matter, energy, information;

B. Transformation;

a. production;

b. facilitation;

c. control and adjustment;

C. Output;

a. identification and assessment;

b. dispatching;

D. Feedback and Adjustment;

a. collecting evidences;

b. analysis and interpretation;

c. constructing adjustment model;

d. stipulating cosequences of adjustment;

e. adjustment introduction;

X. Living Systems:

1. Matter-Energy and Information:

A. Reproducer;

B. Boundary;

2. Matter-Energy:

A. Ingestor;

B. Distributor;

C. Converter;

D. Producer;

E. Matter-Energy Storage;

F. Extruder;

G. Motor;

H. Supporter;

3. Information:

A. Input Transducer;

B. Internal Transducer;

C. Decoder;

D. Channel and Net;

E. Associator;

F. Memory;

G. Decider;

H. Encoder;

I. Output Transducer;

XI. Operations and Their Systems:

1. Input:

I. Matter-Energy and Information:

A. Reproducer;

B. Boundary;

II. Matter-Energy:

A. Ingestor;

B. Distributor;

C. Matter-Energy Storage;

III. Information:

A. Input Transducer;

B. Internal Transducer;

C. Channel and Net;

D. Associator;

E. Memory-Storage;

2. Transformation:

IV. Matter-Energy:

A. Converter;

II. Information:

A. Decoder;

B. Encoder;

3. Output:

I. Matter-Energy:

A. Distributor;

B. Extruder;

II. Information:

A. Output Transducer;

4. Feedback and Adjustment:

I. Matter-Energy:

A. Motor;

II. Information:

A. Decider.

Caveat

The design model presented above fits together as systems within systems. A concentric network of interconnected, trans-sectional, and dynamic systems working together to produce a software, or any design for that matter. The limitation of the human mind remains such that we, as human, reason, understand, and otherwise express ourselves, in a sequential or linear order. This has little to do with reality, except of course, the reality of our minds. But it makes a strong case why we should all become systems thinkers energized by the vision expanding foundation of the systems perspective. We shall next examine a suggested method for measuring the effectiveness of design as creativity. Look out for my next Book in this Series.

"The Rhetorician Ought to Make a Regular Division,

And Acquire a Distinct Notion of Two Classes of Words:

Words With Fluctuating Meaning, and

Words With Steady Meaning.

He Who Made Such a Distinction

Would Have an Excellent Principle."

-Plato-

Comments on Bibliography and References

"In Every Work of Genius We Recognize

Our Own Rejected Thoughts."

-Ralph Waldo Emerson-

Comments on the Bibliography and References

In assembling a Bibliography appropriate to the expanse of the preceding text, I wished to give you, the reader, as broad a perspective as possible on the "Problem of Creativity". Accordingly, the following Bibliography represents a multidisciplinary compendium of titles related to every topic touched upon in this book. While some of these selections appear quite dated, first published in 1888 for example, others proclaim a more recent point-of-view. I included the "ancient" selections to give you, the reader, a taste of the transcendental flavor of the fuller dimensions of the "Problem of Creativity".

The following Bibliography spans disciplines ranging from Systems Philosophy, Psychology, Social Psychology and Systems Science, to Civilizational Ethics, Computer Science, Management Philosophy, Science, and Religion. Topics represented include:

- The Philosophy of Science
- Metaphysics
- Logic
- Human Activity Systems,
- Appreciative Systems

- Evolutionary Guidance
- Software Quality Assurance and Control
- Belief
- Faith
- Mythology
- Reason.

Creativity touches upon all of these. To adequately understand Creativity, one must broaden one's view and see Creativity as more than only an aspect of human personality, an object of investigation. Creativity also must be seen as a "Systems Theme", as a human activity system completely caught up with the concept of design, so much so that design becomes inseparable from creativity itself. The author holds that an understanding of creativity remains impossible without first understanding the expansive domain of transcendental human experience. The following Bibliography illuminates such experience by revealing its progression over the course of the last century. Hence, creativity's legacy becomes not only Philosophy, Psychology, and Systems Science revealed through the theories of academic debate, but also the Management Science, Computer Science, Religion, Belief, Faith and Reason revealed through the light of practical human experience. Hence, the Bibliography suffers in that it must forever remain incomplete.

Bibliography

Ackoff, Russell, L. (1981). Creating The Corporate Future. New York, New York: John Wiley & Sons.

Ackoff, Russell L. & Emery, Fred E. (1972). On Purposeful Systems. Seaside, California: Intersystems Publications.

Adler, Mortimer J. (1980). How To Think About God. New York, New York: Macmillan Publishing Co.

Adorno, T. W. (1967). "Sociology and Psychology". New Left Review, Nov.-Dec., pp. 67-80. (original work published in 1955).

Adorno, T. W. (1968). "Sociology and Psychology II". New Left Review, Jan.-Feb., pp. 79-96. (original work published 1955).

Adorno, T. W. (1978). "Subject-Object". In A Arato & E. Gebhardt (eds.), The Essential Frankfurt School Reader, pp. 497-511. New York, New York: Continuum.

Ainworth-Land, V. (1982). "Imaging and Creativity: An Integrating Perspective." Journal of Creative Behavior, 16, 5-28.

Alberione, Don Giacomo (1971). Carissimi In Sam Paolo. Edited by Rosario F. Esposito, S.S.P. Rome, Italy: Edizioni Paoline.

Amabile, Teresa M. (1983). The Social Psycholoqy of Creativity. New York, New York: Springer-Verlag.

American Educational Research Association (1985). Standards for Educational and Psychological Testing. Washington, D.C.: American Psychologial Association, Inc.

Anderson, James F. (1953). Introduction to The Metaphysics of St. Thomas Aquinas. Chicago, Illinois: Henry Regnery Company.

Anderson, R. G. (1983). Data Processing and Management Information Systems. Estover, Plymouth, England: Macdonald & Evans Ltd.

Angeles, Peter A. (1974). The Problem of God: A Short Introduction. Columbus, Ohio: Charles E. Merrill Publishing Company.

Aristotle, (1941). "Organon". Translated by W.D. Ross, in the Basic Works of Aristotle, edited by R.P. Mckeon. New York, New York: Random House.

Aristotle (1952). Works of Aristotle. edited by W.D. Ross, 12 vols., Oxford, England: Clarendon Press.

Armstrong, A.H. (1949). An Introduction to Ancient Philosophy. New York, New York: Newman Press.

Augustine of Hippo (1981). Basic Writings of St. Augustine. translated by Whitney J. Oates. New York, New York: Baker Books.

Ayer, Alfred Jules (1951). Language, Truth, and Logic, 2nd ed. London, England: V. Gollancy, Ltd.

Ayer, Alfred Jules (1964). "Theology as Meaningless." Edited by J. H. Hicks. From The Existence of God. New York, New York: Macmillan Publishing Company.

Baier, Kurt (1957). The Meaning of Life. Canberra, Australia: Government Printer.

Banathy, Bela H. (1973). Developing A Systems View of Education. Seaside, California: Intersystems Publications.

Banathy, Bela H. (1979). Introduction To Systems Inquiry, Seaside, California: Intersystems Publications.

Banathy, Bela H. (1983). Systems Education: Perspectives, Programs, and Methods. Edited by Banathy. Seaside, California: Intersystems Publications.

Banathy, Bela H. & Armendariz, Joaquin C. (1983). An Exploratory Study of Systemic Design, Chapter Four: Models and Modeling. San Francisco, California: Saybrook University.

Banathy, Bela H. (1984). Systems Design in the Context of Human Activity Systems. San Francisco, California: International Systems Institute.

Banathy, Bela H. (1986). A Review of Design Models. San Francisco, California: International Systems Institute.

Banathy, Bela H. (1987a). The Design, of Evolutionary Guidance Systems. San Francisco, University.

Banathy, Bela H. (1987b). The Characteristics and Acquisition of Evolutionary Competence. San Francisco, California: Saybrook Institute.

Banathy, Bela H. (1987c). Design Inquiry, Vol. I. Edited by Bela Banathy, Ph.D., San Francisco, California: International Systems Institute.

Banathy, Bela (1987). "Design Inquiry In the Context of Human Activity Systems: Design Systems And Systems Models." From Design Inquiry, Vol. I. Edited by Bela Banathy, Ph.D. San Francisco, California: International Systems Institute.

Banathy, Bela H. (1988). "Matching Design Methods to System Type". Systems Research Vol. 5 No. 1, pp. 27-34. Great Britain.

California: Saybrook

Bandas, Rudolph G. (1932). Contemporary Philosophy and Thomistic Principles. Milwaukee, Wisconsin: Bruce Publishing Company.

Barnes, W.H.F. (1950). The Philosophical Predicament. New York, New York: Black.

Barron, F. & Harrington, D.M. (1981). "Creativity, Intelligence, and Personality." Annual Reviews of Psychology, 32, 439-476.

Beardsley, Monroe C. (1960). The European Philosophers from Descartes to Nietzsche. New York, New York: Modern Library.

Bell & Newell (1971). Computer Structures. New York, New York: McGraw-Hill Book Company.

Berger, Peter (1973). The Homeless Mind. New York, New York: Irvington Press.

Berkeley, George (1963). Principles of Human Knowledge. edited by Thomas J. McCormack. New York, New York: Open Court Press.

Berkowitz, Bernard Dr. & Newman, Mildred (1971). How To Be Your Own Best Friend. New York, New York: Ballantine Books.

Berne, Eric, Dr. (1978). Games People Play. New York, New York: Ballantine Books.

Blackham, H. J. (1963). Objections To Humanism. Philadelphia, Pennsylvania: Lippincott.

Bloom, B. S. *1982). The role of gifts and markers in the development of talent. Exceptional Children, 48, 510-522.

Bogdanov, A. (1984). Essays in Tektoloqy: The General Science of Organization. Seaside, California: Intersystems Publications.

Boudlin, Barbara M. (1989). Agents of Change: Managing the Introduction of Automated Tools. Englewood Cliffs, New Jersey: Prentice-Hall, Inc.

Brady, Ignatius (1959). A History of Ancient Philosophy. Milwaukee, Wisconsin: Bruce Publishing Company.

Branden, Nathaniel (1971). The Psychology of Self-Esteem. New York, New York: Bantam Books.

Branden, Nathaniel (1973). The Disowned Self. New York, New York: Bantam Books.

Brennan, Joseph G. (1961). A Handbook of Logic. 2nd edition. New York, New York: Harper & Brothers.

Brill, A.A. (1913). Lectures On Psychoanalysis and Psychology. New York, New York: Arnos Publishers.

Brown, Barbara (1975). New Mind New Body. New York, New York: Bantam Books.

Campbell, D. (1960). "Blind variation and selective retention in creative thought as in other knowledge processes. Psychological Review, 67, 380-400.

Carnap, Rudolph (1935). Philosophical and Logical Syntax. London, England: K. Paul Trench Trubner and Company, Ltd.

Carr, Clay (1989). The New manager's Survival Manual: All The Skills You Need For Success. New York, New York: John Wiley & Sons.

Carroll, Lewis (1956). Symbolic Logic and the Game of Logic. New York, New York: Dover Publications.

Checkland, Peter (1981). Systems Thinking, Systems Practice. New York, New York: John Wiley & Sons.

Christakis, Aleco (1987). "A New Role for Systems Scientist." From the Design Inquiry Series, Vol. I: A Compendium of Selections from the Proceedings of the 1985-1986 Annual Meetings of the Society of General Systems Research. Edited by Bela Banathy. San Francisco, California: International Systems Institute.

Christakis, Alexander N. (1987). "High Technology Participative Design: The Space Based Laser." From Design Inquiry Series, Vol. I. Edited by Bela Banathy, Ph.D. San Francisco, California: International Systems Institute.

Christian, James L. (1981). Philosophy An Introduction into the Art of Wondering. New York, New York: H.R.& W. Publishers.

Churchman, C. West (1989). The Well-Being of Organizations. Edited by Churchman. Seaside, California: Intersystems Publications.

Churchman, C. West (1979). The Systems Approach. New York, New York: Dell Publishing Company.

Clarke, Bowman L. (1966). Language and Natural Theology. The Hague, Netherlands: Mouton & Company.

Collen, Arne (1987a). The Application of Living Systems Process Analysis To Institutional Development in Higher Education. A paper presented at the 31st annual meeting of the International Society for General Systems Research. Budapest, Hungary: June, 1987.

Collen, Arne (1987b). Living Systems Process Analysis for Program Evaluation. A paper presented at the annual meeting of the American Evaluation Association. Boston, Massachusetts: October, 1987.

Collingwood, R. G. (1940). An Essay On Metaphysics. Oxford, England: Clarendon Press.

Conrad, James W. (1989). Handbook of Communications Systems Management. Boston, Massachusetts: Auerbach Publishers.

Conte, Dunsmore, & Shen (1986). Software Engineering Metrics And Models. Menlo Park, California: The Benjamin/Cummings Publishing Company, Inc.

Copi, Irving M. (1978). Introduction To Logic. New York, New York: The Macmillan Company.

Copleston, Frederick, S.J. (1973). Contemporary Philosophy. New York, New York: The Newman Press.

Copleston, Frederick, S.J, (1985). A History of Philosophy, Vol. I: Greece and Rome, Vol. II: Augustine to Scotus, Vol. III: Ockham to Suarez. Image edition. New York, New York: Doubleday.

Copleston, Frederick, S.J. (1985). A History of Philosophy, Vol. IV: Descartes to Leibniz, Vol. V: Hobbes to Hume, Vol. VI: Wolff to Kant. Image edition. New York, New York: Doubleday.

t

Copleston, Frederick, S.J. (1985). A History of Philosophy, Vol. VII: Fichte o Nietzsche, Vol. VIII: Bentham to Russell, Vol. IX: Maine de Biran to Sartre. Image edition. New York, New York: Doubleday.

Coreth, Emerich (1973). Metaphysics. New York, New York: The Seabury Press.

Davis, Gary A. (1986). Creativity Is Forever. Dubuque, Iowa: Kendall/Hunt Publishing Company.

Davis, William S. (1983). Systems Analysis and Design. Reading, Massachusetts: Addison-Wesley Publishing Company.

De Bono, Edward (1985). de Bono's Thinking Course. New York, New York: Facts on File Publications.

De Lubac, Henri (1960). The Discovery of God. New York, New York: P.J. Kenedy and Sons.

Descartes, Rene (1964). The Nature of The Human Mind. Translated by Laurence J. Lafleur. New York, New York: Bobbs Publishing Company.

Dickinson, Brian (1984). Applied Structured Analysis. Brisbane, California: Logical Conclusions, Inc.

Dickinson, Brian (1985). Applied Structured Design. Brisbane, California: Logical Conclusions, Inc.

Dijkstra, E. W. (1976). A Discipline of Programming. Englewood Cliffs, New Jersey: Prentice-Hall.

Dillon, John A., Jr. (1983). Foundations

of General Systems Theory. Seaside, California: Intersystems Publications.

Doctor, R. D. (1972). California's Electric Quandary. California: The Rand Corporation, Vol. 3, September.

Dopp, Joseph M. (1960). Formal Logic. Translated by Robert Ramirez and Robert D. Sweeney. New York, New York: Joseph F. Warner.

Doyle, P. (1976). Every Object is a System. London, England: Interprint Publishers.

Ducasse, C. J. (1953). A Philosophical Scrutiny of Religion. New York, New York: The Ronald Press Company.

Dubos, Rene (1968). So Human an Animal. New York, New York: Charles Scribner's Sons.

Dulles, A. R. et Al (1955). Introductory Metaphysics. New York, New York: Sheed and Ward.

Durant, Will (1961). The Story of Philosophy. New York, New York: Touchstone Books.

Eaton, Ralph M. General Logic. New York, New York: Charles Scribner's Sons.

Eddington, Sir Arthur S. (1929). Science and The Unseen World. London, England: Allen and Unwin.

Eisentadt, J. M. (1978). "Parental Loss and Genius." American Psychologist, 42, 211-223.

Emery, F.E. & Trist, E. L. (1960). "Socio-technical Systems", in C. West Churchman and Michel Cerhulst (eds.), Management Sciences: Models and Techniques, Vol. 2. pp. 83-97. New York, New York: Pergamon Press.

Evans, Michael W. & Marciniak, John J. (1987). Software Quality Assurance & Management. New York, New York: John Wiley & Sons.

Feigenbaum, McCorduck, & Nii (1988). The Rise of The Expert Company. New York, New York: Times Books.

Flew, Antony (1953). A New Approach to Psychical Research. London, England: C.A. Wattes & Company, Ltd.

Flew, Antony (1966). God And Philosophy. New York, New York: Dell Publishing Company, Inc.

Foerster, Heinz von (1984). Observing Systems. Seaside, California: Intersystems Publications.

Foster, Richard N. (1986). Innovation: The Attacker's Advantage. New York, New York:Summit Books.

Foucault, Michael (1973). Madness and Civilization. New York, New York: Random House.

Frankl, Victor (1973). The Doctor and the Soul. New York, New York: Random House.

Freemantle, David (1985). Superboss. London, England: Gower Publishing Company Limited.

Freud, S. (1908). Standard Edition of the Complete Psychological Works of Sigmund Freud, Vol. 9, edited by J. Strachey. London, England: Hogarth Press, 1959.

Fromm, Eric (1959). Psychoanalysis and, Religion. New Haven, Connecticut: Yale University Press.

Gadamer, H. G. (1976). "The Historicity of Understanding". In P. Connerton, Critical Sociology, pp. 117-133. Harmondsworth, England: Penguin Books.

Gadamer, Hans-Georg (1979). Truth and Method. London, England: Sheed and Ward, Ltd.

Gardner, H. (1982). Art, Mind, And Brain: A Cognitive Approach To Creativity. New York, New York: Basic Books.

Garrigou-Lagrange, R. (1934). God, His Existence and Nature. St. Louis, Missouri: St. Louis University Press.

Gasparski, Wojciech (1984). Understanding Design: The Praxiological - Systemic Perspective. Seaside, California: Intersystems Publications.

Getzels, J. W. and Jackson, P.W. (1962). Creativity and Intelligence: Explorations with Gifted Students. New York, New York: Wiley.

Gilson, Etienne (1939). Christianity and Philosophy. London, England: Sheed and Ward.

Gilson, Etienne (1952). Being And Some Philosophers. Toronto, Canada: Pontifical Institute of Mediaeval Studies.

Glasser, William (1965). Reality Therapy. New York, New York: Harper and Row.

Goldstein, M. & Goldstein, I. (1978). How We Know: An Explorations of the Scientific Process. New York, New York: Da Capo press, Inc.

Greer, G. (1979). The Obstacle Race: The Fortunes of Women Painters and Their Work. New York, New York: Farrar Straus Giroux.

Habermas, J. (1971). "Technology and science as 'ideology.'" In J. Habermas, Toward A Rational Society, pp. 21-122. Boston, Massachusetts: Beacon Press.

Habermas, J. (1976). "Systematically distorted communication." In P. Connerton, Critical Sociology, pp. 348-362. Harmondsworth, England: Penguin Books.

Habermas, J. (1980). "The hermeneutic claim to universality." In J. Bleicher, Contemporary Hermeneutics, pp. 181-211. London, England: Routledge & Keagan Paul.

Halberstadt, W.H. (1960). An Introduction to Modern Logic. New York, New York: Harper & Brothers.

Hall, Calvin & Gardner, Lindsey (1978). Theories of Personality. New York, New York: Wiley Publishers.

Harman, Willis, Ph.D. & Rheingold, Howard (1984). Higher Creativity. Los Angeles, California: Jeremey P. Tarcher, Inc.

Harriman, R. (1984, August). "Creativity: Moving Beyond Inner Logic." The Futurist. pp. 17-36.

Hartshorne, Charles (1967). A Natural Theology for Our Times. Lasalle, Illinois: Open Cour Publishing Company.

Hawkins, D.J.B. (1954). Being and Becoming. New York, New York: Sheed and Ward.

Hawkins, D.J.B. (1962). Crucial Problems of Modern Philosophy. South Bend, Indiana: University of Notre Dame Press.

Head, Robert V. (1984). Planning Techniques for Systems Management. Wellesley, Massachusetts: Q.E.D. Information Sciences, Inc.

Hegel, G.W.F. (1979). Philosophy of Religion. Translated by Peter C. Hodgson. New York, New York: Scholars Press Company.

Heisenberg, Werner (1952). Philosophical Problems of Nuclear Science. New York, New York: Pantheon Books, Inc.

Held, David. (1980). Introduction to Critical Theory - Horkheimer to Habermas. Los Angeles, California: University of California Press.

Heraclitus (1954). Fragments. Translated by G.S. Kirk. Cambridge, England: Cambridge University Press.

Horvath, Nicholas A. (1974). Philosophy. Woodbury, New York: Barron's Educational Series.

Howe, M. J. A. (1982). "Biographical Evidence and the Development of Outstanding Individuals." American Psychologist, 17, 1071-1081.

Hunt, Raymond G. (1976). Current Perspective in Social Psychology. New York, New York: Oxford University Press.

Huxley, Aldous (1979). Brave New World. New York, New York: Harper & Row.

Huxley, Julian (1958). Religion Without Revelation. New York, Nedw York: New American Library.

Huxley, T. H. (1894). Science and the Christian Tradition. New York, New York: Appleton & Company.

Jackson (1975). Principles of Program Design. New York, New York: Academic Press.

James, William (1981). Principles of Psychology. Edited by Peter Smith. Boston, Massachusetts: Harvard University Press.

Jastrow, Joseph (1978). God and the Astronomers. New York, New York: W. W. Norton & Company.

Johnson-Laird, Philip N. (1988). The Computer and The Mind. Cambridge, Massachusetts: Harvard University Press.

Johnstone, H. W., Jr. (1954). Elementary Deductive Logic. New York, New York: Thomas Y. Crowell Company.

Jung, Carl G. (1958). The Undiscovered Self. Translated by Little. New York, New York: Atlantic Monthly Press.

Juran, J.M. (1989). Juran on Leadership for Quality: An Executive Handbook. New York, New York: The Free Press.

Kant, Immanuel (1969). The Critique of Pure Reason. Translated by Norman K. Smith. New York, New York: St. Martin Press.

Katsenelinboigen, Aron (1984) Some New Trends in Systems Theory. Seaside, California: Intersytems Publications.

Kaufmann, Walter (1958). Critique of religion and Philosophy. New York, New York: harper & Row.

Kerzner, Harold, Ph.D. (1989). Project Management: A Systems Approach to Planning, Scheduling, and Controlling. New York, New York: Van Nostrand Reinhold.

Keynes, Jogn N. (1906). Studies and Exercises in Formal Logic. 4th edition. London, England: Macmillan and Company.

Klocker, Harry R. (1962). Thomism And Modern Thought. New York, New York: Appleton-Century-Crofts.

Klubertanz, George P. (1955). Introduction To the Philosophy of Being. New York, New York: Appleton¬Century-Crofts.

Kolenda, Konstantin (1976). Religion Without God. Buffalo, New York: Prometheus Books.

Koren, Henry J. (1955). Introduction to the Science of Metaphysics. St. Louis, Missouri: B. Herder Book Company.

Krippner, Stanley (1981). "Access to hidden reserves of the unconscious through dreams in creative problem solving." Journal of Creative, 15, 11-22.

Kung, Hans (1980). Does God Exist? New York, New York: Doubleday & Company, Inc.

Laing, R.D. (1972). The Politics of Experience. New York, New York: Random House.

Lamont, Corliss (1965). The Illusion of Immortality. New York, New York: Frederick Ungar Publishing Company.

Lanyon, Richard L. & Goodstein, Leonard D. (1982). Personality Assessment. New York, New York: John Wiley & Sons.

Le Blanc, Hugues (1957). An Introduction to Deductive Logic. New York, New York: John Wiley and Sons.

Locke, John (1975). An Essay Concerning Human Understanding. Edited by Peter H. Nidditch. New York, New York: Oxford University Press.

Luce, A. A. (1958). Teach Yourself Logic. London, England: The University Press.

Macy, Christopher (1975). Science, Reason,and Religion. Buffalo, New York: Prometheus Books.

Mahoney, James, Ph.D. (1985). The Management Effectivity Analysis. Portland, Maine: Management Research Group.

Maritain, Jacques (1952). Range of Reason. New York, New York: Charles Scribner's Sons.

Maritain, Jacques (1954). Approaches To God. New York, New York: Harper & Brothers.

Maritain, Jacques (1956). Existence and the Existent. Translated by Lewis Galantiere and Gerald B. Phelan. Garden City, New Jersey: Image Books.

Maritain, Jacques (1957). An Introduction to Logic. New York, New York: Sheed and Ward.

Martin, C.B. (1959). Religious Belief. Ithaca, New York: Cornell University Press.

Martin, James (1967). Design of Real-Time Computer Systems. Englewood Cliffs, New Jersey: Prentice-Hall.

Martin, Malachi (1976). Hostage to the Devil. New York, New York: Reader's Digest Press.

Mascall, E. L. (1949). Existence and Analogy. London, England: Longmans, Green And Company.

Matson, Wallace I. (1965). The Existence of God. Ithaca, New York: Cornell University Press.

May, Rollo (1975). The Courage to Create. New York, New York: Bantam Books.

Mayon-White, Bill & Morris, Dick (1982). Systems Behavior: Module 1 Systems and how to describe them. Walton Hall, Milton Keynes, Great Britain: Open University Press.

Mclean (1976). The Human Side of Systems: The User's Perspective. Los Angeles, California: Western Systems Conference.

McNamara, Curt (1987). "Designing The Future: The Possibility-Space and the Information Environment." From the Design Inquiry Series, Vol. I. Edited by Bela Banathy, Ph.D. San Francisco, California: International Systems Institute.

McPherson, Thomas (1965). The Philosophy of Religion. London, England: D. Van Nostrand Company, Ltd.

Mednick, S.A. (1962). "The associative basis of the creative process". Psychological Review, 69, 220-232.

Merker, Stephen L. (1985). "Living Systems Theory: A Framework for Management." Article in Behavioral

Science, Vol. 30, pp. 187-194.

Miller, Edgar (1972). Clinical Neuropsychology. New York, New York: Wiley.

Miller, James G. (1978). Living Systems. New York, New York: McGraw-Hill Book Company.

Mises, Richard Von (1951). Positivism: A Study in Human Understanding. Cambridge, Massachusetts: Harvard University Press.

Misiak, Henryk & Sexton, Virginia S. (1966). History of Psychology. New York, New York: Grune.

Mitchell, Basil (1957). Faith and Logic'. Boston, Massachusetts: Beacon Press.

Monsma, John Clover (1958). The Evidence of God in an Expanding Universe. New York, New York: Putnam.

Montagu, Ashley (1974). The Natural Superiority of Women. New York, New York: Macmillian Publishing Company.

Moore, Edward Caldwell (1936). The Nature of Religion. New York, New York: Macmillan.

Morgan, C. L. (1923). Emergent Evolution. London. England: Williams and Norgate.

Mourant, John A. (1963). Formal Logic. New York, New York: Macmillan Company.

Muller, Max (1903). Theosophy. London, England: Longmans, Green, and Company.

Murray, John C. (1964). The Problem of God. New Haven, Conn: Yale University press.

Myers, Glenford (1979). The Art of Software Testing. New York, New York: John Wiley & Sons.

Nadler, Gerald (1987). "An Assessment of Systems Methodology and Design." From Design Inquiry Series, Vol. I. Edited by Bela Banathy, Ph.D. San Francisco, California: International Systems Institute.

Nagel, Ernest (1954). Sovereign Reason. Glencoe, Illinois: The Free Press.

National Institute of Business Management (1988). Executive Skills Enrichment. New York, New York: National Institute of Business Management.

Negoita, Constantin Virgil & Ralescu, Dan (1987). Simulation, Knowledge-Based Computing, and Fuzzy Statistics. New York, New York: Van Nostrand Company, Inc.

Nevius, Warren Nelson (1941). Religion As Experience and Truth. Philadelphia, Pennsylvania: Westminster Press.

Newkirk, Raymond L. (1976). The Chronicles of The Making of a Philosopher: Book V-1, In Defense of Reason. Fort Lauderdale, Florida: (Unpublished Manuscript).

Newkirk, Raymond L. (1976a). The Chronicles of The Making of a Philosopher: Book V-2, In Defense of Reason. Fort Lauderdale, Florida: (Unpublished Manuscript).

Newkirk, Raymond L. (1976b). Chronicles of The Making of a Philosopher: Book III, Theodicy. Fort Lauderdale, Florida: (Unpublished Manuscript).

Newkirk, Raymond L. (1982). The Chronicles of The Making of a Philosopher: Book II, What Is Philosophy?

Newkirk, Raymond L. (1987). A Systems Models Description of a Software Development System. Pleasant Hill, California: (Unpublished Manuscript).

Fort Lauderdale, Florida: (Master Thesis, Columbia Pacific University).

Newkirk, Raymond L. (1988). A Comprehensive Characterization and Description of the Software Development Human Activity System. Pleasant Hill, California: (Unpublished Manuscript).

Newkirk, Raymond L. (1988a). Systems Design. Pleasant Hill, California: (Unpublished Manuscript).

Newkirk, Raymond L. (1988b). A Description of the Software Development Human Activity System. Pleasant Hill, California: (Unpublished Manuscript).

Newkirk, Raymond L. (1988c). A Project Proposal for the Design of a Computer Software Development Human Activity System. Pleasant Hill, California: (Unpublished Manuscript).

Newkirk, Raymond L. (1988d). The Nature and Characteristics of Human Activity Systems in General and The Computer Software Development Human Activity In Particular. Pleasant Hill, California: (Unpublished Manuscript).

Newkirk, Raymond L. (1988e). Speculations About Methods or Approaches Used to Work with the Computer Software Development Human Activity System. Manila, Philippine Islands: (Unpublished Manuscript).

Newkirk, Raymond L. (1988f). Some Distinctions Between a Systems Approach and Other Methods of Disciplined Inquiry. Pleasant Hill, California: (Unpublished Manuscript).

Newkirk, Raymond L. (1988g). Reflections on Emergence and Holsim. Pleasant Hill, California: (Unpublished Manuscript).

Newkirk, Raymond L. (1988h). The Observer Defines the System. Pleasant Hill, California: (Unpublished Manuscript).

Newkirk, Raymond L. (1989). A Revised Approach for The Design of the Software Development Human Activity System. Pleasant Hill, California.

Newman, John Henry (1939). An Essay in Aid of Ascent. London, England: Longmans, Green & Company.

Nersoyan, H. J. (1969). The Theism of An Atheist. Syracuse, New York: Syracuse University Press.

Nicholson, John A. (1950). Philosophy of Religion. New York, New York: Ronald Press.

Nielsen, Kai (1971). Contemporary Critiques of Religion. New York, New York: Herder and Herder, Inc.

Noonan, John P. (1957). General Metaphysics. Chicago, Illinois: Loyola University Press.

Olle, T. William et Al (1988). Information Systems Methodologies: A Framework for Understanding. New York, New York: Addison-Wesley Publishing Company.

Oman, John (1931). The Natural and The Supernatural. Cambridge, England: Cambridge University Press.

Open Systems Group (1983). Systems Behavior. Edited by the Open Systems Group. London, England: Harper & Row, Publishers.

Orr, K. T. (1982). Structured Requirements Definition. Topeka, Kansas: Ken Orr & Associates, Inc.

Ortega, Jose Y Gasset (1932). The Revolt of the Masses. New York, New York: Norton Press.

Otto, Rudolph (1931). The Philosophy of Religion. London, England: Williams and Norgate.

Otto, Rudolph (1950). The Idea of The Holy. Oxford, England: Oxford University Press.

Page-Jone, Meilir (1980). The Practical Guide to Structured Systems Design. New York, New York: Yourdon Press.

Page-Jone, Meilir (1985). Practical Project Management. New York, New York: Dorset House Publishing.

Paton, Herbert James (1955). The Modern Predicament. New York, New York: Macmillan.

Patterson, William (1926). The Nature of Religion. New York, New York: Doran.

Bibliography

Perls, Frederick S. (1971). Gestalt Therapy Verbatim. New York, New York: Bantam Books.

Perry, William E. (1981). Effective Methods of EDP Quality Assurance. Wellesley, Massachusetts: Q.E.D. Information Sciences, Inc.

Perry, William E. (1988). A Structured Approach to Systems Testing. 2nd edition. Wellesley, Massachusetts: Q.E.D. Information Science, Inc.

Pfeiderer, Otto (1888). The Philosophy of Religion on The Basis of Its History. London, England: Williams and Norgate.

Phillips, Debora (1978). How To Fall Out of Love. Boston, Massachusetts: Houghton Mifflin Company.

Plantinga, Alvin (1967). God And Other Minds: A Study of The Rational Justification of Belief in God. Ithaca, New York: Cornell University Press.

Plantinga, Alvin (1978). The Nature of Necessity. New York, New York: Oxford University Press.

Plutarch (1975). The Lives of the Great Greeks. Translated by Ian Scott-Kilvert. New York, New York: Penguin Books.

Polkinghorne, Donald (1983). Methodology for the Human Sciences. Albany, New York: State University of New York Press.

Pollard, William G. (1958). Chance and Providence. New York, New York: Scribner.

Pontifex, Mark & Trethowan, Illtyd (1953). Meaning of Existence. London, England: Longmans, Green & Company.

Prior, A. N. (1955). Formal Logic. Oxford, England: Oxford University Press.

Pratt, James Bissett (1931). Adventures In Philosophy and Religion. New York, New York: Macmillan.

Radhakrishnan, S. (1947). Religion and Society. London, England: Allen and Unwin.

Rahmatian, Sasan (1987). "The Boomerang Effect: A Design Principle for Human Activity Systems." From the Design Inquiry Series, Vol. I. A Compendium of Selections from the Proceedings of the 1985-1986 Annual Meetings of the Society of General Systems Research. Edited by Bela Banathy, Ph.D., San Francisco, California: International Systems Institute.

Rahner, Karl (1973). On The Theology of Death. New York, New York: Seabury Press.

Rand, Ayn (1961). For The New Intellectual. New York, New York: New American Library.

Rapoport, Vladimir S. (1987). "Complex Relationships AS A Subject-Matter of Management Systems Analysis and Design." From Design Inquiry Series, Vol. I. Edited by Bela Banathy, Ph.D., San Francisco, California: International Systems Institute.

Ray, Michael & Myers, Rochelle (1986). Creativity In Business. New York, New York: Doubleday.

Reich, Charles (1970). The Greening of America. New York, New York: Random House.

Reik, Theodor (1951). Dogma and Compulsion. New York, New York: International Universities Press.

Rice, A.K. (1963). The Enterprise and Its Environment. London, England: Tavistock Publications.

Robbins, Rossell Hope (1959). The Encyclopedia of Witchcraft and Demonology. New York, New York: Crown Publishers, Inc.

Ross, D. T. (1980). Software Engineering. New York, New York: Academic Press.

Roszak, Theodore (1973). Where The Wasteland Ends. New York, New York: Doubleday.

Royce, Josiah (1902). The Conception of God. New York, New York: Macmillan Publishing Company.

Royce, Josiah (1906). Studies of Good and Evil. New York, New York: Appleton.

Runes, Dagobert (1967). The Treasury of Philosophy. Totowa, New Jersey: Littlefield, Adams & Company.

Runes, Dagobert (1972). Dictionary of Philosophy. Totowa, New Jersey: Littlefield, Adams & Company.

Russell, Bertrand (1935). Religion and Science. London, England: Oxford University Press.

Russell, Bertrand (1940). History of Western Philosophical Thought. London, England: George Allen & Unwin, Ltd.

Russell, Bertrand (1949). Mysticism and Logic. London, England: G. Allen and Unwin.

Sabatier, Auguste (1906). Outlines of A Philosophy of Religion. London, England: Hodder and Stoughton.

Sagan, Carl (1973). The Cosmic Connection. New York, New York: Doubleday.

Sampson, E. E. (1981). "Cognitive Psychology As Ideology". From the American Psychologist, 36, pp. 730-743.

Sampson, Edward E. (1983). Justice and the Critique of Pure Reason. New York, New York: Plenum Press.

Sander, Donald H. (1981). Computers In Business. New York, New York: McGraw-Hill Book Company.

Santayana, George (1955). Skepticism and Animal Faith. New York, New York: Dover Publications.

Schank, Roger (1988). The Creative Attitude. New York, New York: Macmillan Publishing Company.

Sellers, Roy Wood (1918). The Next Step in Religion. New York, New York: The Macmillan Company.

Semprevivo, Philip C. (1982). Systems Analysis Definition, Process, And Design. Chicago, Illinois: Science Research Associates, Inc.

Seth, P. & Andres, P. (1920). The Idea of God. Oxford, England: Oxford University Press.

Sheldon, Wilmon Henry (1954). God and Polarity. New Haven, Connecticut: Yale University Press.

Sillem, Edward (1961). Ways of Thinking About God. New York, New York: Sheed and Ward.

Siu, R.G.H. (1958). The Tao of Science. Cambridge, Massachusetts: M.I.T. Press.

Skinner, B. F. (1953). Science and Human Behavior. New York, New York: Free Press.

Skinner, B. F. (1971). Beyond Freedom And Dignity. New York, New York: Alfred Knopf.

Smith, Vincent E. (1950). Idea-Men of Today. Milwaukee: Wisconsin: Bruce Publishing Company.

Sorley, W. R. (1919). Moral Values and The Idea of God. Cambridge, England: Cambridge University Press.

Sprague, Elmer (1961). What Is Philosophy? New York, New York: Oxford University Press.

Stace, Walter Terence (1952). Religion and The Modern Mind. Philadelphia, Pennsylvania: Lippincott.

Stamps, Jeffrey S. (1980). Holonomy. Seaside, California: Intersystems Publications.

Stebbing, L. Susan (1961). A Modern Introduction to Logic. New York, New York: Harper & Brothers.

Stevick, E. L. (1971). "An empirical investigation of the experience of anger." In A. Giorgi, W. F. Fischer, & R. Von Eckartsberg, Duquesne Studies in Phenomenological Psychology: Volume 1, pp. 132-148. Pittsburgh, Pennsylvania: Duquesne University Press.

Stewart, Hugh B. (1989). Recollecting The Future. Homewood, Illinois: Dow Jones-Irwin

Stoll, Robert R. (1961). Sets, Logic and Axiomatic Theory. San Francisco, California: W.H. Freeman and Company.

Suarez, Francis (1947). "On the Various Kinds of Distinctions." Translated by Cyril Vollert in Disputationes Metaphysicae, Disposition 7. Milwaukee, Wisconsin: Marquette University Press.

Sullivan, Daniel J. (1957). An Introduction to Philosophy. Milwaukee, Wisconsin: Bruce publishing Company.

Sundgren, B. (1975). Theory of Data Bases. New York, New York: Petrocelli-Charter.

Taylor, Alfred E. (1947). Does God Exist? New York, New York: Macmillan Publishing Company.

Temple, William (1951). Nature, Man and God. London, England: Macmillan.

Tennant, F. R. (1930). Philosophical Theology. Cambridge, England: Cambridge University Press.

Thierauf (1973). Data Processing for Business and Management. New York, New York: John Wiley & Sons.

Thomas Aquinas, St. (1948). On Being And Essence. Translated by Armand Maurer. Toronto, Canada: Pontifical Institute of Mediaeval Studies.

Thomas Aquinas, St. (1963). Summa Theologiae. Edited by Blackfriars. New York, New York: McGraw-Hill Book Company.

Thompson, John B. (1984). Study In The Theories of Ideology. Berkeley, California: University of California Press.

Thompson, Samuel Martim (1955). A Modern Philosophy of Religion. Chicago, Illinois: Regnery.

Thompson, William (1972). At The Edge of History. New York, New York: Harper and Row.

Thrower, James (1975). A Short History of Western Atheism. Buffalo, New York: Prometheus Books.

Toffler, Alvin (1971). Future Shock. New York, New York: Bantam Books.

Toynbee, Arnold (1961). History of Man. New York, New York: Oxford University Press.

Trueblood, David Elton (1942). The Logic of Belief. New York, New York: Harper.

Trueblood, David Elton (1957). Philosophy of Religion. New York, New York: Harper.

Tsanoff, Radoslav A. (1924). The Problem of Immortality. New York, New York: Macmillan.

Wadsworth (1973). The Human Side of Data Processing Management. Englewood Cliffs, New Jersey: Prentice Hall.

Walshe, T. J. (1933). Quest of Reality. St. Louis, Missouri: B. Herder Book, Company.

Walton, Mary (1986). The Deming Management Method. New York, New York: Putnam Publishing Company.

Ward, James (1915). Naturalism and Agnosticism. London, England: Black.

Ward, Leo R. (1935). Values and Reality. New York, New York: Sheed and Ward.

Warfield, John N. (1987). "On The Choice for Frames for Systems Studies." From the Proceedings of the 1985¬1986 Annual Meetings of the Society of General Systems Research. Edited by Bela Banathy, Ph.D., San Francisco, California: International Systems Institute.

Watkin, Edward Ingram (1936). Theism, Agnosticism, and Theism. London, England: Unicorn Press.

Watson, J. B. (1970). Behaviorism. New York, New York: Norton Library.

Watson, John (1907). The Philosophical Basis of Religion. Glasgow, Scotland: Maclehose.

Webb, C.C.J. (1911). Problems in the Relations of God and Man. London, England: Nisbet.

Webb, C.C.J. (1915). Studies In the History of Natural Theology. Oxford, England: Oxford University Press.

Weiss, Paul (1950). Man's Freedom. New Haven, Connecticut: Yale University Press.

Whitehead, Alfred N. (1929). Process and Reality. New York, New York: Macmillan Publishing Company.

Whitehead, Alfred N. & Russell, Bertrand (1962). Principia Mathematica. New York, New York: Cambridge University Press.

Wiederhold, Gio (1977). Data Base Design. New York, New York: McGraw-Hill Book Company.

Wieman, Henry Nelson (1936). American Philosophies of Religion. Chicago, Illinois: Willett Clark.

Windelband, Wilhelm (1950). History of Ancient Philosophy. New York, New York: Dover Publications.

Wisdom, John (1964). "The Modes of Thought and the Logic of God." Edited by J. H. Hick from The Existence of God. New York, New York: Macmillan Publishing

Company.

Witten, I.H. (1982). Principles of Computer London, England: Academic Press.

Wittgenstein, L. (1953). Philosophical Investigations. New York, New York: Macmillan.

Wittgenstein, L. (1961). Tractatus Logico¬Philosophicus. London, England: Routedge & Kegan Paul.

Wobbermin, George (1953). The Nature of Religion. New York, New York: Crowell.

Wolfson, Harry A. (1956). The Philosophy of The Church Fathers. Cambridge, Massachusetts: Harvard University Press.

Wright, William K. (1958). Student's Philosophy of Religion. New York, New York: Macmillan.

Wylie, Philip (1979). Generation of Vipers. New York New York: The Larlin Corporation.

Yourdon, Edward (1978). Structured Design. New York, New York: Yourdon Press.

Yourdon, Edward (1989). Structured Walkthroughs.2nd. ed. Englewood Cliffs, New Jersey: Prentice-Hall, Inc.

Ziff, P. (1959). "The Feelings of Robots." Analysis, 19, 64-68. (353).

Zimmer, Heinrich (1971). The King and The Corpse. Princeton, New Jersey: Princeton University Press.

Zuriff, G. E. (1985). Behaviorism: A Conceptual Reconstruction. New York, New York: Columbia University Press.

Zuurdeeg, Willem F. (1958). An Analytical Philosophy of Religion. New York, New York: Abingdon Press.

Books are the Territory of The Mind

and

The Rich Fruit of Courageous Dreams.

-Raymond L. Newkirk -

Research and Development

We pursue our systems research and development activities to support contract delivery within the enterprise architecture and information systems domains using the SMI Systems Architecture.

Systems

Architecture

Systems Philosophy

General Theory of Systems

Self-Systems Psychology

Appreciative Systems

Evolutionary Guidance Systems

Design Inquiry

Human Activity Systems

Living Systems Theory

Systems Methodology

Systems Analysis

Systems Behavior

Living Systems Process Analysis

Management and Education

Expanded Systems Visioning

Formal Systems Development

Methodological Network

Systems Change Management Process

Self-Systems Development Process

Systems/Project Management

Intelligence Systems Development

Leadership Support Systems

Human Activity Systems Environment

Infrastructure Design

Systems Implementation Planning For

Full Systems R & D

Systems Integrity Design

Systems Training

PAX ET BONUM

Don't miss out!

Visit the website below and you can sign up to receive emails whenever Dr. Raymond Leslie Newkirk publishes a new book. There's no charge and no obligation.

https://books2read.com/r/B-A-HJRKE-IMBQJ

Did you love *The Creativity Myth*? Then you should read *A Person Passing By*[1] by Dr. Raymond Leslie Newkirk!

[2]

This work emerged from a lifetime of experience assisting organizations, teams, and individuals with finding inventive ways to solve problems more rapidly. As you move from country to country and culture to culture in search of inventive solutions to problems that are more common than one would ever imagine, you begin to notice several patterns emerge that reduce some of the mystery that shrouds the nature and character of human relationships including: How we form them; how we manage them; how we end them, and how we overcome them. This is the stuff of life. Life is relationship living. In Christianity, we believe in God as Relationship. If you ask how I describe human life, I will answer you this way: Life is Relationship. For

---

1. https://books2read.com/u/3kzRnN

2. https://books2read.com/u/3kzRnN

good or bad, from hope to hopelessness, from self-doubt to confidence, from Ego to Self-Esteem, and from life to death, I would tell you that human life is formed, nourished, developed, enjoyed, and even made miserable through relationship, from birth to death. From the day you meet your mother to the day you meet your undertaker; you pass through life in relationship.

How you manage your relationships says everything about how you will become a fully human person imbued with the capacity for living a life of significance. We are creatures with the capacity to reason well, true; but human life is considerably more emotional than rational. Rationality is the power we possess to navigate life on a material planet. However, we feel more than we think. We use reason occasionally to assist in decision-making but use our emotions most often to navigate the experiences of our lives. Think about this: Reason concerns the rules of logic, but emotion flows from the values we hold dear. Emotions represent value judgments, and reason represents logical conclusions, if-then-else. The decisions we make based on value judgements often conflict with the decisions we conclude from deduction or induction. This is how human life is lived on planet earth. I am not so sure.

www.ingramcontent.com/pod-product-compliance
Lightning Source LLC
LaVergne TN
LVHW100140061126
851857LV00010B/175
9798235426160